Post-Traumatic

Stress Disorder

**Carolyn Simpson and
Dwain Simpson L.C.S.W.**

THE ROSEN PUBLISHING GROUP, INC./NEW YORK

Post-Traumatic

Stress Disorder

**Carolyn Simpson and
Dwain Simpson L.C.S.W.**

THE ROSEN PUBLISHING GROUP, INC./NEW YORK

Published in 1997 by The Rosen Publishing Group, Inc.
29 East 21st Street, New York, NY 10010

First Edition

Library of Congress Cataloging-in-Publication Data
Simpson, Carolyn.
    Coping with post-traumatic stress disorder / Carolyn Simpson and
Dwain Simpson.
        p.   cm. — (Coping)
    Includes bibliographical references and index.
    Summary: Discusses such situations as physical abuse, natural
disasters, wars, and violence, that can cause stressful responses and
describes ways of dealing with these delayed reactions to trauma.
    ISBN 0-8239-2080-1 (lib. bdg.)
    1. Post-traumatic stress disorder—Juvenile literature. [1. Post-
traumatic stress disorder.] I. Simpson, Dwain, 1951–.
II. Title. III. Series.
RC552.P67S456   1997
616.85′21—dc21   96-52619
                                                                               CIP
                                                                                AC

Acknowledgments

Special thanks to Janet Hueners for her help in the planning of this book. Her
candor and willingness to share her stories have been important to our work.
    Thanks, too, to Helen Chamberlain, a psychologist in Oklahoma City, for her
advice regarding trauma victims and their families. And to Sam Shehab for his
insight into chronically traumatized cities, specifically Beirut, Lebanon.

ABOUT THE AUTHORS ◇

Carolyn Simpson currently teaches psychology at Tulsa Junior College, in Tulsa, Oklahoma. She received her Bachelor's degree in sociology from Colby College, in Waterville, Maine, and her Master's degree in human relations from the University of Oklahoma. In addition to being a teacher, she has been a clinical social worker in both Maine and Oklahoma.

Dwain Simpson is a licensed clinical social worker employed by Tulsa Regional Medical Center. He also works in private practice in Tulsa, Oklahoma. He received both his Bachelor's degree in political science and his Master's in social work from the University of Oklahoma. He has practiced social work for more than eighteen years.

The authors have collaborated on two previous books: *Careers in Social Work* and *Coping with Emotional Disorders*. Mrs. Simpson has written ten other books on health-related issues.

The couple reside with their three children on the outskirts of Tulsa.

Contents

Introduction

Paul served in the Vietnam war more than twenty-five years ago. He never talked about his war experiences when he got back, even with his wife. As far as he was concerned, it was all behind him.

Nobody knew Paul was still troubled by his war experiences. One day, ten years after he had returned home, he was reading the paper in his living room. His wife was turning on the stereo. Suddenly, the room shook, as a house down the street from them burst into flames.

Paul knocked over the couch and ducked behind it for cover. "Get my gun," he called to his wife, though it wasn't his wife he was seeing then; it was other servicemen from the war.

"Take cover," he called, and he sat trembling on the floor. He expected another grenade to come flying in through the window any minute.

By the time Paul and his wife learned that a gas leak had caused their neighbor's house to explode, Paul had calmed down. "I guess I should tell you about the war," he said to his wife. "I thought the shelling was starting again."

A classroom of third-graders gathered around a television set on January 28, 1986. They watched in awe as the space shuttle *Challenger* lifted off, soaring into the air with a teacher aboard. Seconds later, the space shuttle exploded, leaving only plumes of smoke shooting off in different directions. The kids didn't understand what had happened at first. Was the space shuttle supposed to do that? Where was it now?

Their teacher was so shocked that she just stood and watched. Over and over, the news kept playing those last few seconds. The space shuttle lifted off just like the others before it. And then, poof! It was gone.

When it dawned on the teacher that the people aboard the space shuttle had died, she shut off the television. But shutting off the television did not keep the third-graders from replaying the disaster in their minds.

Some kids held out, hoping that the crew members had parachuted to safety, but that was really implausible. Everyone had died, and people worldwide had watched it happen.

Most of the time, people hear about post-traumatic stress disorder (PTSD) and assume that the victim is a combat veteran. While wartime vets initially brought this disorder to our attention, they are far from the only ones to experience symptoms. The third-graders who watched the space shuttle explode on national television were also affected by PTSD. Anyone who has been in a car accident or has been caught in the crossfire of rival gangs likely suffers from PTSD too. Those who have been abused over a long period of time suffer even more intensely.

In 1980, the American Psychiatric Association included for the first time the category of post-traumatic stress disorder in its official diagnostic manual of mental disorders. PTSD is a stressed reaction to a traumatic event, such as being held hostage, being sexually or physically abused, or seeing loved ones burned in a fire or battered by a rampaging tornado.

The basic symptoms of PTSD are similar in response to any kind of traumatic event. Children and adults suffer alike, although kids are not as prone to suffering flashbacks. All, in varying degrees, suffer from hyperarousal (always being on guard against danger), intrusion (thinking about the traumatic experience over and over, or trying not to think about it at all), and constriction (numbing your thoughts and avoiding others so you do not relive the traumatic event).

This book looks at the different events, such as war, disasters, abuse, captivity, and violence, that can lead to PTSD. Some experiences lead to more alarming symptoms, such as trancelike behavior, and others provoke symptoms that don't occur until many years later. But what is important to remember is that PTSD is a treatable condition. You can get better once you are ready to deal with the memories of the traumatic event. That is the good news; the bad news is that you will never heal if you simply pretend that the trauma never took place, or that it wasn't bad enough to warrant such anxiety on your part. Our memories play tricks on us, distorting time and sequence, but rarely do they materialize out of nowhere. And while they may go underground for weeks, months, or even years, they never completely go away.

It is necessary to confront your traumatic memories to get on with your life. If you know what to expect when confronting your memories, you'll be better able to tolerate the anxiety that goes along with them. It is to that end—educating you about PTSD—that we've written this book.

SITUATIONS CAUSING PTSD

CHAPTER 1

Natural Disasters

O ne winter evening, as twilight was turning to darkness, our neighbor's house went up in flames. We heard the woman's screams before we saw flames or smelled smoke. Everyone had escaped from the house and stood huddled together on the front lawn, while Mrs. Anderson kept screaming over and over. It was a frightening sound, a wail of both horror and despair.

Then we saw the fire. The windows exploded and orange flames erupted, climbing the house. Though smoke filled the air and our lungs, all we could see were flames. They were devouring the house. Family members wrung their hands, and Mrs. Anderson kept screaming.

Fire trucks arrived within minutes, but the fire had too strong a grip on the house, and firefighters could only keep it from spreading to other houses. Our neighborhood watched as the house burned right to the ground. Nothing was saved; the family escaped only with the clothes on their backs.

Days later in a nearby park, we found scraps of notebooks and blackened pictures belonging to the Anderson family. Watching their things blow through the neighborhood was a terrible reminder for everyone of the tragic fire. It must have been additionally horrifying for this family to see their partially burned belongings circulating through the neighborhood. Though this family had not been hurt physically, they had lost many things that they held dear.

Some people are not so lucky in fires. Richard was badly disfigured in a fire that destroyed the house he was renting. The furnace had blown up as a result of faulty installation. At twenty-one, Richard sustained burns over 90 percent of his body. He was rushed to a local medical center, where doctors initially told him that he would die. They even urged him to call his family to say his goodbyes. But he did not die, and as he clung to life, doctors transferred him to a special burn hospital where Richard's health improved.

When Richard began seeing a counselor, he was badly disfigured from the fire. Repeated skin grafts had left his face with discolored skin. The fire (and subsequent grafts) had altered his appearance to such a degree that Richard had trouble accepting who he was. He suffered from nightmares in which his house blew up all over again, and he was engulfed in flames. Again and again he was frightened, told he would die, and was operated on in his dreams that would not go away.

Years ago, a tornado ripped through Tulsa, Oklahoma, leaving a wide path of destruction down I-44. It leveled a truckstop, threw cars around the highway, and ripped the roofs off several houses that stood in its way. Worse than that, it killed many people.

Tornadoes are powerful wind storms that are cold, dark, and unpredictable, and grab at everything in their paths. People who live in tornado-prone areas in the country are usually watchful during tornado season, but this tornado caught even the meteorologists by surprise. They had only ten minutes to warn the public.

People traveling on I-44 who weren't listening to local radio stations were at a disadvantage. If they did not know what tornado sirens sounded like, they did not know to get off the road and into a ditch or under an overpass. Most of the people killed by this tornado were from out of state. A family from Chicago was killed when they spotted the tornado too late. Strong winds lifted their car and tossed it across the road. Only one child survived, and she was taken to a local hospital to recuperate with strangers. Relatives arrived days later to take her back to Chicago. Imagine this little girl's terror at seeing the looming tornado, waking up alone and injured in an unfamiliar hospital, and being told that the rest of her family had been killed.

Janet and I graduated from college together in Maine and later settled in different parts of the country. I ended up in Oklahoma; she ended up in Los Angeles. She tried to get me to come visit, but I was always afraid of earthquakes. Janet wasn't worried about earthquakes; they happened all the time, and she assured me that "you get used to them."

"But what about the big one?" I would ask. "The one that's coming?"

"It's not coming in my lifetime," she would say.

That is what our conversations sounded like until January, 1994, when California was hit by a massive earthquake. Sylmar, California (a suburb of Los Angeles), where Janet lived, was virtually on fire.

I finally got through to Janet via the telephone and confirmed that she was okay, but the repeated aftershocks were taking a toll on her house and her emotions. She told me what happened.

About 4:30 in the morning while asleep on her waterbed, she was awakened by what she thought was a mini tidal wave in her waterbed. Being groggy with sleep, it took her a few seconds to realize that the movement was not from her husband tossing and turning on the bed; it was from an earthquake. She and her husband, Derek, raced to the baby's room, while their six-year-old son, Adam, lay in his bed stiff with fear. Janet made a detour back to Adam's room when she realized Derek had Amy safely in his arms. Then the four of them huddled in the doorway of the living room to wait out the tremors. They could hear the rumbling of the quake grow in intensity the closer it got. It lasted only thirty seconds or so, but "thirty seconds can be the longest time of your life," Janet told me. "It seems never-ending, especially when you don't know it's going to end in thirty seconds."

Janet and her family escaped, physically unharmed. Their house sustained only minor cosmetic damage, but the continuing aftershocks in the days that followed kept the trauma alive for them all. Every little tremor made Janet wonder, "Is this the big one?"

Within seven months, Janet (who had lived in Los Angeles for twenty years) had moved her family clear across the country to Atlanta, Georgia.

Hurricane Andrew is considered one of the most devastating natural disasters to occur in U.S. history. When it struck the southern part of Dade County in Florida in August 1992, people were unprepared for its ferocity. Hurricanes had hit there before, but not with 200 m.p.h. winds. Winds that high can smash through windows that aren't adequately boarded up, and once they get in, they can rip the roof off and suck household contents into the air.

As survivors ventured outside following the storm, they saw virtually every house in their neighborhoods reduced to rubble. Many people lost their homes, their boats, and all of their belongings. For those who weren't insured, they lost most of their lifetime investments.

The hurricane affected people in many ways. Some had nightmares that the hurricane returned, others became anxious every time the clouds darkened the sky, thinking Andrew had come back.

HOW PTSD AFFECTS A PERSON

Horrible experiences create permanent mental pictures. They are frightening and traumatic, and our minds play them over and over again for us. If we try to push them aside, they come back in dreams and nightmares to haunt us.

Shock and utter helplessness combine to make the brain automatically imprint these memories. And not just the memories, but all the feelings that accompanied the trauma at the time. Because of the mind's capacity to remember and relive the experience, people with post-traumatic stress disorder suffer from three major symptoms.

The first symptom is **hyperarousal**. People who have suffered a traumatic experience will startle easily, react irritably to things that would not ordinarily bother them, and sleep poorly. Some people cannot fall asleep and others fall asleep but can't stay asleep for very long. They startle themselves awake over every inconsequential noise in the house. It is as if these people are always on the alert for danger to strike.

You can imagine how loud noises must affect Richard, the man who was burned when his furnace blew up. Janet's daughter who experienced the earthquake is now fearful of big machines that make loud noises; bulldozers and helicopters particularly scare her. Janet no longer sleeps eight hours per night. She wrote me, "I'm not consciously worrying or nervous, but I just don't sleep." She also mentioned that she still cannot get herself "to turn the light off at night no matter how tired" she is.

Janet also stopped reading for almost eight months. The act of reading requires someone to relax enough to escape into the book's story. Janet could not let her guard down long enough to read even a page. Though she did not realize she was "still on the alert," that apparent vigilance kept her from relaxing enough to read a good book.

Many people who survived Hurricane Andrew worried each time the weather turned stormy. Even though no hurricane was forecast, they expected the worst.

The second symptom of PTSD is **intrusion**, or when a person keeps reliving the trauma. Bad memories are not always that easy to dismiss. People have **flashbacks**: they see the whole event happening in their minds and believe they are experiencing it again. Janet drifted off to sleep one evening and thought she heard the earthquake coming again. Many combat veterans hear noises or see things that trigger their memories, and they start reexperiencing the whole event. When Paul heard the house down the street blow up, he thought he was back in Vietnam in the midst of battling the Vietcong. He did not realize that he was safe in his house in the suburbs.

Younger people do not seem to have flashbacks because they tend to daydream about, and thus consciously re-experience, the trauma they have suffered. Many kids who survived Hurricane Andrew relived the storm every day. They drew pictures of the destruction, and they readily compared stories with their classmates. Older adolescents and adults, who perhaps are trying to forget the memories, are more prone to having flashbacks.

Intrusion occurs when the memory of the trauma keeps reinserting itself in the victim's awareness. People suffering from PTSD don't just have nightmares; they have repetitive nightmares and repetitive dreams. The nightmares may not all be exactly alike, but the themes will be the same. Children usually play out their traumas over and over without understanding what they are doing. Several children who had been kidnapped and buried alive back in the 1980s later played "kidnapper tag" with their friends. Others kept burying their Barbie dolls or taking them for rides on "kidnapped vans." This kind of repetitive play is called **reenacting** the trauma; it is obsessive and monotonous. Older people may reenact their traumas by getting into relationships that duplicate the abuse in their pasts.

The third PTSD symptom is **constriction**. This literally means "numbing." Because the memories are so intrusive, people resort to different tactics to be able to tolerate this assault. Some people just turn off their feelings. Someone cannot wipe away a memory that the brain has automatically imprinted, but she *can* numb herself to the feelings that were stored along with the memory. The bad thing about turning off feelings is that someone cannot selectively turn off the "scary or sad" feelings and hang onto good feelings. If someone numbs himself, he loses *all* feelings. Many people with PTSD seem to be flat; they do not show excitement, happiness, or joy because they have numbed themselves to sadness, horror, and fear.

Likewise, in an attempt to create some safety in their lives and to manage their fears, many traumatized people restrict their lives. They avoid everything that might trigger their bad memories, and they avoid relationships because it hurts to love and lose people.

People with PTSD suffer from a variety of feelings: shame, guilt, and anger. Janet suffers from tremendous guilt because Adam was left alone in the initial seconds of the earthquake, because both she and her husband thought to grab the baby first. The neighbors whose house had burned down had just cleaned their fireplace, and stored the ashes in a trash bag in the garage. The smouldering ashes had caused the fire. If only they had stored them in a metal container outside. If only they had not cleaned the fireplace. If only. . . .

Richard is furious with his landlord for the faulty installation of the furnace, and he is angry at God for letting him suffer. He is mad at people who stare at him and at the doctors who saved him. His anger bubbles up over everything and stems from having had no control over what happened.

People who have witnessed others dying during a disaster have to work through the stages of grief, in addition to their feelings about the trauma. Grieving time is not the same for everyone. At first, survivors experience shock and denial. They tell themselves the tragic event did not happen, or that it was not really so bad. Shock eventually gives way to anger, as if their outrage can undo the injustice of what happened. Anger covers the sadness and recognition of the loss. Once the loss is mourned, it can be accepted. The victim is then ready to get on with his or her life.

CONSEQUENCES OF PTSD FOR THE SELF

Sleep disorders are very common with victims of PTSD. People suffer either from **insomnia** (the inability to fall asleep or stay asleep) or nightmares. If they cannot get any rest at night, they will probably become jittery, irritable, and/or impulsive.

Some individuals become anxious or depressed. Those who spend their time worrying about the trauma and trying to avoid its recurrence belong to the first category. Those who give in to a feeling of helplessness are depressed.

Many times victims succumb to free-floating anger. Adam (Janet's son) had a lot of trouble controlling his anger in the months following the earthquake. He began playing rough on the playground at school and did not pay attention to the teachers. He had not figured out how to handle his feelings about the disaster and was lashing out at everyone.

Studies of Vietnam veterans treated for PTSD show that men who keep to themselves were likely to become irritable and short-tempered after their stints in battle. Paul probably fit into that category. After he returned from Vietnam, he would frequently put his fist through glass when angered. Once, while driving to work, he got mad at a motorist who cut in front of him. Angry but unable to vent it on the motorist, he punched the window out in his own car.

Vietnam vets who were more compassionate and moralistic upon entering the war suffered more from depression afterward. These were men who had been forced to compromise their values. Unable to accept what they had done, they became depressed and disgusted with themselves.

Paranoia is another PTSD symptom, in which a person may seem unjustly suspicious. People who are paranoid may seem unusually jumpy, because they are always on guard for another disaster. Victims of weather-related catastrophes may come to fear the weather conditions that precipitated the disaster. People traumatized by tornadoes often get panicky when dark clouds loom on the horizon or a sudden cold gust of wind stirs the leaves on the trees. Janet decided to move out of California because she could not tolerate the aftershocks and constant reminders of the earthquake. People who have survived fires are nervous around flames, even when the fire is safely confined to a fireplace.

Being anxious all of the time is nerve-wracking and hard on your body. Victims of PTSD suffer overwhelmingly from ulcers, high blood pressure, and—if they have turned to drugs and alcohol to help alleviate their pain—the physical complications of substance abuse. Drugs, including alcohol, have a numbing effect on emotions. Unfortunately, they cause more problems, such as addiction and liver disease. People often turn to drugs to suppress the immediate feelings of panic in the aftermath of a trauma. Initially, these substances cause fear and anxiety to go away, and victims mistake these reactions for relief. Soon, they need to use more drugs to maintain the reprieve. They may become addicted, actually needing the alcohol or drug to keep from facing the pain of withdrawal. But addiction has its own set of problems. Alcoholics face DTs (a scary condition in which the victim feels as if bugs are all over his body), liver disease, and other stomach problems. People can drink themselves to death. Drug addicts require increasing amounts of the drug to control their symptoms, but they can die when taking too much of a substance. Once they get to this point, it's too painful to stop on their own and too dangerous to continue.

The physical sensations a person experiences during a trauma may continue to afflict the person in future stressful situations. For example, if you experienced a crippling stomachache while you watched your house burn down, you are likely to suffer similar stomachaches each time you face stress. If you woke up with a headache after a tornado ravaged your neighborhood, you might find yourself getting headaches during stressful conditions. These physical symptoms that flare up after a trauma are called **psychophysiologic signs**.

Lastly, people who suffer from PTSD can lose their will to live. If severely traumatized, the victim may come to believe that he has no control over his life. Feeling out of control can cause hopelessness about the future. He may say to himself, "Why should I work hard and have hope for the future when I have no control over what happens in my life?" This thinking could even lead to suicide.

CONSEQUENCES OF PTSD FOR FAMILY AND FRIENDS

PTSD has the greatest impact on relationships. It is hard to maintain a relationship with a traumatized person. She either clings tenaciously to the loved one, fearing she will lose him, or else purposefully pushes the loved one away because she feels that he hasn't lived up to her expectations. Richard had an especially difficult time with relationships. Since he did not like himself because he had a disfigured face, he did not expect others to find him likable either. If women went out with him, he hated himself afterward for "needing" them so much. He assumed that they felt sorry for him, and he spurned them. In his initial rage, he could not seem to get beyond his disfigurement, and he blamed everyone else for the feelings he really had himself.

Some people find themselves reconnecting with lost family members after a tragedy, but others get caught up in their anger. They blame survivors for surviving; they hold rescuers accountable for the tragedy itself. Friends of victims need to be prepared to prove their loyalty and love over and over again to the trauma victim. The victim no longer believes he has any control over his life. He makes up for this realization by either controlling everyone around him or by withdrawing. He may feel that he cannot trust anyone in this world. As a result, the victim brings bitterness and disillusionment to all of his relationships.

Some victims even turn against their loved ones, especially if the disaster resulted in their child's death or injury. Each blames the other because there is no satisfaction in cursing an act of nature. In a way, guilt serves a purpose because it makes the victim believe she really did have some control over the event. If only she had turned on the radio, she would have known a tornado was coming. If only they had made a plan of action in case of fire, they would have all gotten out safely. If only he had not stayed home from church that morning, he would not have been burned. Blaming yourself and others will not help the situation; it will make matters worse by tearing apart good and loving relationships. It is better to realize that you have little control over external events and begin rebuilding your life.

Rape, Sexual, and Physical Trauma

People suffer trauma even at the hands of those they love. Many years ago I was treating a woman named Maria for depression. She was too tired to prepare meals and often went to bed after the evening meal her daughter prepared. She worked a few hours a day outside the home but increasingly found herself unable to take care of her own house. More and more, she retired to her bedroom, shutting out her husband and kids.

Gradually, her teenage daughter began to take her place. Nelda cooked the meals and cleaned up afterward. She sat up late keeping her father company watching television. She laughed at his jokes and cuddled with him on the couch. Maria didn't seem to notice or to care.

Maria's husband began to view their daughter as a wife. He forbade Nelda to go out on dates and boarded up her bedroom window so she couldn't sneak out at night. He monitored her comings and goings after school. Soon enough, he started going into her room at night, supposedly "to tuck her in."

By the time Maria found out what was going on, her husband had been sexually abusing their daughter for several months. As incredulous and disgusted as Maria was, she was terrified that her husband would be thrown in jail. She begged her daughter to "forget about it all" and promised things would get better.

Nelda was furious—both at her dad for betraying the father/daughter bond, and at her mother for not seeing the abuse as the trauma that it was. She felt used by both of them. Initially, Nelda was afraid to talk about the abuse with anyone. Bitter and ashamed, she withdrew from her friends and eventually tried to commit suicide.

Another woman I treated named Caron said she was not sexually abused; but she had all the symptoms of PTSD. As a child, she was encouraged by her father to bring friends home. At first her father would treat them all to ice cream. Caron liked this special attention from her dad. Then he would take them riding in his car out to the country. Inevitably, he would stop the car, climb in the back seat with her friends, and molest them; Caron would get out and wander around outside. She suspected he was doing "bad things" to her friends, but she felt responsible for having brought them over in the first place. Feeling guilty and scared, Caron started withdrawing. Though she never talked about it with her dad, she stopped bringing her friends home and eventually "forgot" what used to happen to them.

Though Caron tried to forget all the details, years later she became more and more depressed and anxious as her own daughters got older. Part of her remembered what her father had done years ago, and she still saw herself as a helpless little girl who had helped her father do terrible things. Caron now worried that similar things might happen to her own daughters.

In 1972, Janet and two other college acquaintances rented a house for the summer. The three of them moved into the house in June and took jobs as waitresses at a nearby military base. One night after a late dinner, Janet and Andrea sat down to watch television while Pam washed her hair in the kitchen sink.

Three-quarters of the way into the TV show, a man holding a T-shirt in front of his face slipped into the house through their unlocked back door and surprised Pam in the kitchen. Waving a gun in the direction of the family room, he ordered Pam to go get her friends. When Pam didn't move, the man strode into the family room himself and told the women to get into the kitchen and turn off all the lights.

Janet initially thought the guy was someone from college playing a practical joke on them. She quickly realized this wasn't a prank and tried not to look at the man, believing that she wouldn't be able to identify him later and so he would not try to kill her. The man separated the women, putting Janet and Andrea in a back bedroom. He stayed with Pam in the family room. Janet strained to hear what was going on; she thought he was there to rob them, and if they all just did as he said, he'd take their jewelry and run. She heard Pamela scream, and then the gunman hit her and cursed.

Why didn't Janet and Andrea run for help? Much like others in the midst of a life-threatening event, they feared they would be killed if they didn't do as the gunman wanted. They huddled in the bedroom and waited.

Within minutes, the gunman called to Andrea. Janet was now alone in the bedroom, still straining to hear everything the man said. When she heard him order Andrea to take off her underwear, she realized the man was there to rape them. Janet heard more screaming and crying and hoped he wouldn't kill them.

Suddenly, she heard the back door slam shut. It took a few minutes before Janet dared leave the bedroom. The other women had been raped, and Pam's face was bruised, but they were both alive.

Panicked and afraid to have a lot of strange men in the house, no one dared call the police. They called their landlord, who lived across the street, and he eventually called the police.

The police were unsympathetic at first, challenging the women's stories. The police wondered why no one had gone for help and why they had been so compliant.

Janet struggled to explain that they all thought they were going to be killed and that they had been paralyzed with fear when they saw no other choice.

Both Andrea and Pam left their jobs and returned to their families. Janet was the only one to finish out the summer in the house. She was terrified of every little noise and had the landlord put locks on all the doors and windows. She believed that if she did not overcome her fear that summer, she would live with it the rest of her life. She made it through the summer, but even now, she sometimes gets anxious being alone at night.

Janet may not have been physically raped that night, but in her mind she had already submitted. She was traumatized by the fear of being killed and from witnessing her friends being raped. In addition to that, she was burdened with survivor's guilt, the feeling that she didn't have the right to be upset because nothing bad had actually happened to her. Convinced her fright and despair were unjustified, Janet fought to keep the feelings hidden and tried to bury the memories.

Physical abuse can be just as frightening and humiliating as sexual abuse, especially if it happens over a period of time. I once treated a young man named Wesley who had been beaten by his alcoholic father throughout his childhood. Though he stood six feet tall, Wesley still thought of himself as a little boy and was intimidated by his father. When Wesley was smaller, his father would literally pick him up and throw him against the wall. He would throw hot coffee on the boy, and if he didn't like his dinner, he would dump the food on the boy's head.

Wesley endured this humiliation and blamed his father's behavior on the alcohol. He loved his father dearly, which made it impossible for Wesley to hold him accountable for the abuse. So Wesley blamed himself, thinking that if he could please his father, then his dad would stop hitting him.

Wesley felt he would never please his father and grew depressed and fearful around others. He was afraid of his father, and he was disgusted with himself. When I first saw him, Wesley would cringe when he heard others shouting. He kept his chair far away from mine, as if he expected me to come at him. Wesley suffered from PTSD, but the trauma was not a one-time event. He suffered from repeated trauma, a series of events that continued to frighten and humiliate him.

Rape is a life-threatening event. Because the victim thinks that he or she is going to die, or feels humiliated enough to want to die, she or he experiences the same type of symptoms as the combat veteran suffering from PTSD. A survivor can be forever "on alert" for danger, and may lose faith in the basic goodness of the world. She or he starts avoiding certain places and certain people, and gradually starts to feel constricted and numb.

A single-event trauma, such as Janet's, is usually re-called vividly. In times of stress, the brain automatically imprints and stores a frightening memory. Twenty years after the rapes, Janet still recalls every detail of that night, including the TV show she was watching. The memory doesn't change with time.

Repeated trauma is different, however. People who have been chronically traumatized (physically or sexually abused over a period of time) repress more of their expe-riences. They have to deaden themselves to their feelings of rage, helplessness, and shame or they wouldn't be able to survive. Once abuse becomes a pattern, victims usually know when it is coming, and they use tricks to persuade themselves that it isn't happening or that it isn't that bad. To make matters worse, the perpetrators of these crimes confuse their victims by convincing them that they are acting out of love and concern. One client confessed that her parents would come home drunk several nights a week and her stepfather would have sex with her, explain-ing that this was how parents taught their kids about sex. Physically abusive parents try to convince their children that they deserve this mistreatment. And children, who desperately want to love and be loved, eventually believe that they *are* at fault and deserve what they get. This makes it more difficult for them to try to stop the abuse. Instead of questioning the adults, they question themselves.

A WORD ABOUT MEMORIES

Before we look at why repeated trauma is different from single-event trauma, let's look at how memories are formed and kept. Remembering information has three parts: first, you must perceive something happening. (If people can convince themselves that something isn't significant, the brain won't remember it.) Second, the brain stores the information in a variety of places. The more places the information is stored (different sensations are stored in different parts of the brain), the more likely it will be retained. Finally, the brain has to retrieve the information.

When something profoundly shocking happens, we usually remember it without even trying. Can you recall where you were when you heard that the Federal building in Oklahoma City had been blown up? Our sense of position (where we were at any given time) is particularly keen in an automatic memory. Just as television gives us instant replays, our minds do the same thing with traumatic memories, until we can't seem to get the images out of our minds. Of course, the more you **rehearse** a memory (think about it or talk about it), the more securely it gets stored.

Have you ever awakened from a disturbing dream and immediately told someone about it? The next day, that dream was easier to recall because you had already "rehearsed" it by talking about it. If you wake up, note the dream, but then fall back asleep, chances are you won't recall many details in the morning. That's because the dream wasn't rehearsed. The same thing applies to studying. The subjects you study the hardest are usually the ones you remember the best. The material you forget to go over ahead of time is usually the hardest to recall.

With a single-event trauma, the memory recalls the event over and over. A repeated trauma is different, though. A child could not survive replaying instances of physical and sexual abuse (particularly at the hands of a loved one). If a child is abused by a parent, who can he turn to for support? If his parent treats him like this, who will love him? A child has no one else and no other resources. He can not live with the memory of these experiences, particularly when they are ongoing. He has to turn his memory off.

How do you stop the memories? Some people simply stop thinking about them. **Suppression** is the conscious act of not thinking about something. People may run away from their feelings and thoughts, but know the bad feelings are still there. You certainly remember that you flunked a math test, but you choose not to think about it.

Repression is different. The person does not do this consciously; he or she simply stops rehearsing the memory and it doesn't get stored in one's memory very well. Or he denies reality by thinking "this isn't happening." If the person does not perceive something happening, it won't be significant enough to be remembered. And if he works hard enough initially to cast the thought aside, he soon "forgets" that it ever happened.

Suppressed and repressed memories are still there, though, and when tapped into, they can usually be recovered in full. Children choose other ways, however, to lose their memories. They enter trancelike states.

At the time something very painful is happening to a child, he or she will enter another world where the pain doesn't exist. Some chronically abused kids count the dots on ceiling tiles while they are being abused. Other children repeat certain phrases over and over, "I'm okay, I'm okay," as a parent advances to hit them.

When I was pregnant with our first child, my husband Dwain and I took natural childbirth classes. To overcome the pain of childbirth, we learned to focus on something else. To teach us how hard it was to do, our instructor gave each of us a small bowl of water with ice cubes in it. We were told to put our whole hand in the bowl of ice water and leave it there for a full minute. When the ice started to hurt our hands, we were supposed to focus on something else and disregard the pain.

I plunged my hand into the ice cold water and glanced at the clock. This wasn't too bad, I thought. I tried not to concentrate on the clock, but when my fingers started to burn and ache, I looked up. Only ten seconds had gone by. The burning became intense, but I knew labor was going to be worse. I kept my hand still. My whole hand started cramping, and all I wanted to do was yank it out and wrap it in a warm towel. Only fifteen seconds had gone by. I knew then that I had to think about something else or I'd never make it. I imagined myself at the ocean and the sun was beating down on me, warming my skin. I strained to see the seagulls flying overhead and the departing ships in the distance. I tried to visualize the waves crashing against the rocks. My hand was no longer a part of me, and I didn't feel it hurting. Soon I heard the instructor saying, "Okay, take your hands out of the water, ladies." Every single woman there had managed to survive the minute. Each one of us had had to go "somewhere else" in our heads to ignore the pain.

While dissociative states are helpful because they keep the person unaware of the trauma, they can be dangerous. Pain serves a purpose. It tells us something is wrong and needs to be fixed. If you learn to ignore the pain, you don't do anything positive to end it. If your mind goes somewhere else when you're being abused, you are still being abused. While you may be less aware of it, the trauma still continues.

It takes a bit of effort to dissociate in the beginning, but eventually, it becomes almost automatic. Memories are still stored, but in fragments. Sometimes the brain retains most of the memory but loses the worst or most conflicted part. Many who claim not to remember certain parts of their childhood may have used dissociation in the past to cope. Unfortunately, children who go into trances to avoid pain discover that they lose their ability to tolerate any strong emotion. They end up being "emotionless" kids.

The most extreme practitioner of dissociation is the victim of **dissociative identity disorder**. This person splits off into entirely separate people, not just personalities, when he or she dissociates. These separate people, called **alters**, protect him or her from the chronic trauma (usually sexual abuse). The danger, of course, is that the original person gets lost among the alters, losing the capacity to integrate the alters' knowledge, emotions, and memories.

People diagnosed with dissociative identity disorder have two or more alters, or parts of their personalities, who act like separate individuals. Each has a different style of behavior, different mannerisms, and different speech patterns. Some can even be sick (running fevers) at the same time that other alters are not. Initially, the "host personality" (the person we know as Susan, for example) is unaware of these other people. All she may know is that she is missing blocks of time. Her friends may think that these different personalities are really Susan, but Susan won't be able to remember doing the things they describe.

One alter may have suffered the abuse for her, which means that Susan has no memory of the abuse. Another alter may behave aggressively because Susan isn't able to. So whenever aggression is called for, this other alter takes Susan's place and Susan effectively sleeps through the changes. Other aspects of her personality come forth as alters, and each of them recalls only what happens to them. That makes it hard for the host to realize everything that has happened to her.

HOW MEMORIES RETURN

Traumatic memories do not deteriorate much, even if they are repressed or not consciously thought about. A person can go a number of years without being bothered by the traumatic event. The traumatic memories are stored away.

The structure of the brain has something to do with memory storage. The human brain has four lobes on each side, and each of the lobes has different functions. Long-term memory is located in one place, memory for spatial relationships and physical sensations is located in another, and visual memories and emotions are located in yet another area. Because memories are in more than one place, they are particularly resistant to being totally erased. They can be recovered in different ways, depending on what sense you tap into. Visual cues are the quickest way to retrieve a memory. Seeing something might trigger a memory of something you thought you had forgotten long ago. Sometimes having a child the same age as you were when the trauma happened will cause a memory to surface. Sometimes, being in the same place will bring the memory back.

Josh was a seven-year-old boy who had gone to spend the night at his best friend's house. At some point during the evening, the friend's babysitter pulled Josh's pants down and teased him about his Mickey Mouse underwear. Josh was both embarrassed and confused. He didn't like what the babysitter was doing, but he didn't think she would quit even if he asked her to. Later, this babysitter held Josh up by his ankles, so her friend (another teenager) could have a look at his Mickey Mouse shorts. Josh ran off and hid; he later developed a stomachache and went home.

Josh seemed to have worked through his trauma. He talked about this babysitter (who apparently hadn't realized how abusive her behavior had been), and he avoided going over to his friend's house when she was there. He didn't spend the night with his friend for several months. When he finally spent the night again, he called home at midnight. Even though the babysitter wasn't there, Josh felt her presence and got his stomachache all over again. Being in the same house at night brought the memory of her teasing back to mind.

When people dissociate, however, their trancelike states do not allow detailed memories to form. Nevertheless, memories still form, even if they are hazy and in fragments. Sometimes, only the memory of the "feelings" is stored; the event itself is never stored. People have to trust their feelings when trying to figure out if a returning memory is true or not.

Sometimes memories return once the abuser dies. The victim may not recall having been abused until the death and then starts having vague recollections.

A person who has been traumatized shows signs and symptoms of trauma. Even if she can't remember the specific circumstances, she reenacts the trauma in her play or in her relationships. She is likely to have recurrent nightmares and psychophysiological symptoms, like Josh's stomachache the second time he tried to spend the night at his friend's house.

CONSEQUENCES OF PTSD FOR THE SELF

The victim of physical and sexual trauma experiences the same symptoms of PTSD as the victim of a disaster. He is helpless, angry, anxious, and alert to danger around every corner. The victim of repeated abuse experiences more of these symptoms as he starts to recall his traumas.

The victim of sexual abuse often feels an enormous amount of humiliation. She sees herself as dirty and frequently has sleep disorders, either insomnia or nightmares. If the abuse took place during the night, the victim may have trouble getting to sleep and staying asleep, even if she can't recall the abuse. Her body remembers even if she dissociates from the trauma, and knows that night is a dangerous time.

Victims of physical and sexual abuse have repetitive dreams and tend to reenact their traumas in obsessive play. If a trained professional were to observe them, she would probably be able to guess the nature of the trauma.

People who try to bury their traumatic memories often become substance abusers, because drugs and alcohol can numb the pain. Unfortunately, substance abuse creates additional problems.

Chronically abused children lose their sense of a future; they do not see themselves growing old. They don't pic-

ture themselves as happily married grandparents, sur-
rounded by doting grandchildren. Instead, they see their
lives ending prematurely. Their worldview already has
encompassed many bad things.

People who dissociate in order to cope with repeated
trauma risk losing themselves. Some children physically
hurt themselves to aid the dissociative process or to bring
themselves back from a trance. Either way, these children
carve on their arms, burn themselves with cigarettes,
or stick themselves with sharp instruments. This self-
mutilating behavior becomes a coping mechanism.

People with dissociative identity disorder have an especially turbulent time. They lose blocks of time (when different alters take over their bodies) and often engage in
self-destructive behavior. Different alters may seek to reenact the trauma by becoming promiscuous. Other alters
may want to get rid of the host, believing her to be too
weak to function in their best interest.

Whether it has been a single-event trauma or repeated
trauma, the victim still suffers the three cardinal signs of
PTSD: hyperarousal (the victim is always attuned to danger); intrusion (the victim remembers vague feelings if
not the trauma outright); and constriction (the victim
seeks to forget through dissociating and avoiding people
and places reminiscent of the trauma).

CONSEQUENCES OF PTSD FOR
FAMILY AND FRIENDS

Victims of prolonged abuse understandably have trouble
with relationships. They have a tendency to trust too
much or too little. The psychologist Erik Erikson noted
that a person must negotiate several developmental mile-
stones on his way to adulthood. The first task for the infant

is learning to trust. Understandably, the abused child never masters this developmental task. The child who fails to develop trust tends to bestow it haphazardly on others and ends up being hurt.

The abused child likewise never masters the developmental tasks of initiative and competence. If he has been abused, whether physically or sexually, he learns not to trust his environment and not to do things for himself because he feels inept. If you see yourself as incompetent, you have to depend on others for the rest of your life. And if you don't trust anyone, you're going to be miserable needing people you can't trust.

Victims can't trust others not to hurt them, and that includes loved ones. It's hard for them to relax in any relationship. They perceive sexual threats even when none exists or they sexualize relationships simply because that is how they have grown up relating to people.

As a result, chronically traumatized people have boundary problems with others. They tend to see others as either all good or all bad. They see everyone as a potential rescuer, and they are inevitably disappointed in most. This may go back to the way they felt about the people in their lives who did not put a stop to their abuse or did not stop it soon enough.

One young woman started seeing a therapist and decided in the first session that she had the most wonderful therapist in the world. She idolized her and found herself wanting to spend more and more time around her. After a while, she invited the therapist to her house for dinner. The therapist declined, telling her that their relationship took place in the office. The young woman became angry and saw the therapist as someone who had never really cared for her. She skipped her next appointment and then called the office to request a change in therapists.

Idolizing someone one minute and then despising them the next usually occurs when people fail to live up to the expectations of trauma victims. But it is hard to correct this behavior because trauma victims have trouble seeing both the good and the bad in one person.

People with boundary problems (expecting too much from a person) scare off a lot of people with their intense feelings. They are also prone to having trouble expressing their sexual needs in an appropriate relationship, usually because they never learned how to express themselves in a healthy relationship.

People who have been raped have a great deal of trouble engaging in sex again. Even though they choose their partner and consent to sex in the future, the act of intercourse is reminiscent of the trauma.

And finally, chronically abused trauma victims have a tendency to reenact their traumas by getting into unstable relationships or by taking care of their abuser later in life. One of my former clients had her stepfather move in with her when her mother died. She claimed he had nowhere else to go and she felt sorry for him. This man had sexually abused her and was a verbally abusive alcoholic. Margaret housed, fed, and humored her stepfather until he died. She never could explain why. She simply had a need to stay connected to this man, even though he had been abusive to her in the past.

CHAPTER ◇ 3

Wars and Captivity

Perhaps you have a parent who served in the Vietnam war. Many veterans suffered from PTSD from this war. Their horrible experiences during the war were compounded by the weak support received from American citizens. Many veterans were reluctant to talk about their experiences. They worked hard to forget what had happened to them over there; as a result many became substance abusers, having started their abuse during the war.

Combat soldiers face death every moment of their tour of duty. They may become dehumanized by all of the killing. The adrenalin rush a soldier experiences during war is hard to turn off, even when he safely returns home. Remember, he has lived with the idea of being tortured and killed for the duration of his duty. Many veterans suffer flashbacks and still see danger lurking around every corner. One man, a former veteran of war, recalls thinking that little kids shooting off firecrackers on July 4th were snipers on the rooftops.

Journalist Terry Anderson was the longest-held American hostage in the Middle East. He was captured by Muslim extremists in March 1985 and not released until December 1991. Amazingly, he survived in reasonably good mental health, despite being chained to a wall during most of his captivity. While he was afraid of being killed at first, he was mostly afraid of never seeing his family again. His guards would raise his hopes of being released, and then dash them, leaving him to doubt that they ever meant to release him.

At times his captors would isolate him; they would take away his radio, cutting him off from everyone. He was humiliated, forced to use the bathroom only once a day (at their whim, not his need), and use a bottle the rest of the time. He couldn't bathe regularly or wear clean clothes. These circumstances can take away someone's dignity.

Fortunately, Terry Anderson retained his dignity by resisting in small ways and reconnecting to a higher power. He survived almost seven years of mistreatment. This is not to say he did not have his share of fearful moments, irritability, and utter despair.

Holding someone against his will clearly takes away his sense of control. This is repeated trauma, and the captive held a long time may resort to dissociation to help him survive.

Patty Hearst was kidnapped in the 1970s. Her captors, the Symbionese Liberation Army, threw her blindfolded into a closet and kept her there for a month. They fed her, but she could eat only with her blindfold on. They escorted her to the bathroom, where she had to use the toilet in the presence of her escort. Stripped of dignity and her connections to the rest of the world, and led to believe they would kill her at any moment, Patty initially lost the will to live. When offered the chance to join her captors, she saw that as a way of staying alive.

Patty eventually did things she never imagined doing. She taped nasty messages that were sent to her parents, had sex with her various kidnappers, and ultimately helped them rob a bank. This last act convinced her that she had gone over the edge and was no longer worthy of rescue.

Patty Hearst's story does end on a positive note. She was finally captured, and though imprisoned for her part in the bank robbery, was eventually pardoned. Most people realized she had acted so bizarrely because of her ongoing trauma. People who are overwhelmed, threatened, and rendered helpless are prone to doing whatever it takes to stay alive. And even when safe, the trauma memories linger: Patty's home is now protected by an elaborate security system.

In July 1976, kidnappers seized a busload of children from Chowchilla, California, on their way home from summer school. They forced the children and their bus driver to get into two vans, drove them to a location eleven hours away, and then buried them all in a huge underground trailer. This event showed the world that tremendous shock can lead to immobilization and compliance. No one had resisted. Fortunately, two older boys and the bus driver dug the way out for everyone and were later rescued by police.

Although the children had been missing for about twenty-four hours, and no one had died, they were all greatly traumatized by the kidnapping. Some kids felt guilty that they did not do something, even though their captors had guns. Others were angry—at themselves for being on the bus, at their parents for sending them to school that day, and at the police for not rescuing them sooner. Surprisingly, they focused more anger on the rescuers than on the captors themselves. Most were satisfied that the "bad guys" were caught and imprisoned, though many still feared the kidnappers would return to harm them in the future. The Chowchilla kidnapping showed the world how trauma affects children.

HOW PTSD AFFECTS THE PERSON

Some captives in Beirut with Terry Anderson fared better than others. Another captive, Terry Waite, remained in isolation most of his years in captivity. Alone and unstimulated, he suffered from many symptoms of PTSD.

Captives suffer the same symptoms of hyperarousal, intrusion, and constriction as anyone else experiencing PTSD. Most hostages left Beirut once they were released from captivity. Others increased security around themselves and their loved ones.

With combat or other veterans, the most talked-about symptoms are flashbacks. Most vets don't want to remember their friends' deaths or the enemy soldiers they killed. They need to forget these experiences, but the mind has already stored the memories. While they consciously suppress the material, the memories surface in the form of flashbacks and nightmares. The trauma is too great to lie quietly in the back of one's mind. When something evokes the memory, such as a visual cue or a certain smell, the trauma seems to come flooding back and is usually much more than the victim can handle at one moment.

Children who have been kidnapped replay the events in their minds. They also prefer to think that they were in control of the situation as it makes them less vulnerable that way. While children can recall their traumas vividly, they tend to distort time. Unaware of what they are doing, they rethink the trauma and insert things beforehand that really happened *after the trauma*. Then, when they tell the story, they actually believe that their trauma was forecast; they just didn't pay attention to the warnings. This makes them feel that they could have had more control over the event.

For example, one girl in the Chowchilla kidnapping remembered getting a call the morning of the kidnapping that mentioned that something bad would happen. Actually, the call came days after the girl was safely back at home. By reinserting the phone call to the day of the kidnapping, the girl convinced herself that she had paranormal powers and could have prevented her abduction if she had only listened. That way, things were not so unpredictable.

Wishing is something else that distorts what the traumatized child remembers seeing. Part of memory is perceiving the information. If it is misperceived, it will be stored as such. Some traumatized people *want* to see things a certain way and, already distressed to such a degree, actually end up distorting the real information. These misperceptions become stored as the memory.

When our daughter was almost three years old, tornado sirens sounded in the middle of the night. That meant a tornado had been sighted in our area and we were in immediate danger. We grabbed Michal and her baby sister and dragged mattresses into our hallway—the safest spot in our house. We heard the tornado coming; it sounded like a freight train bearing down on us. The wind rose around our house, but the sky became oddly still. All we could hear was that train coming. Michal knew we were scared and knew that something dangerous was happening around us.

Fortunately the tornado skipped over our house; it never touched down. When the danger had passed, we calmed the children and put them back to bed. To this day, Michal talks about the tornado that came through our hallway. In her mind, it sailed right down the middle of our house because that is where she remembers us hiding.

A person's sense of time distorts when remembering a traumatic event. Lengthy events seem shorter; short, scary events seem longer. You have probably noticed that boring or scary events seem to last forever, while happier times fly by. It is the same with trauma. A single, scary moment is prolonged because the victim has no idea when it is going to end. When that earthquake threatened Janet and her family, she tried to explain why those thirty seconds seemed like hours. Likewise, when her friends were raped and she sat in the darkened room, she thought the rapist had been there an hour or so. It had only been ten minutes.

The opposite happens during prolonged trauma. Captives are usually surprised to find that more time has gone by than they expect. This is another trick of the mind. If people were truly aware of every second ticking past, they would lose hope in rescue. People without hope lose their will to live; thus, this shortening of time increases the chance of victims being able to "hang in there." They simply have no idea how long they have been traumatized.

CONSEQUENCES OF PTSD FOR THE SELF

Former hostages startle more easily than other people, and they acquire more mundane fears of the dark, strangers, loud noises, or deep water. However, people who have been traumatized remain afraid of these things well into adulthood—long after nontraumatized children have outgrown their fears. Even though they were not trauma-tized in the dark, they may now be afraid of the dark. They simply develop ordinary fears after having experienced a trauma, usually captivity, and react strongly to these feelings.

Hostages, including combat veterans who are in a sense hostages to the war, experience shame, guilt, and help-lessness. That's exactly what captors want their victims to feel because they know these emotions break the hos-tage's will to resist. Victims feel especially degraded and often lose hope when they have been forced to commit atrocities or hurt others to save themselves.

These people especially have no sense of a future; they don't care about living a long life because they can't envi-sion surviving a long time with these memories. Children may give up on their dreams and behave self-destructively or they may take up a risky hobby, such as motorcycle racing. Some start hanging out with a questionable crowd. Young women may drop out of school to get married at an unusually early age.

Many hostages develop substance abuse problems (as do combat veterans) because it seems like a quick fix to obliterate the pain. Most don't drink to relax; they drink to forget what has happened to them. Children don't neces-sarily turn into alcoholics right after a trauma, but they're likely to experiment with drugs as a way to avoid their feelings. They may eventually turn to alcohol, simply be-cause it's a more socially acceptable way of escape in this society.

Some people develop other psychological disorders under the stress of prolonged captivity. One of the hostag-es with Terry Anderson appeared to be hallucinating and was barely coherent at times. Several years after his release he was finally hospitalized for mental problems, including paranoia and delusions compounded by substance abuse.

Some people manage to continue living a regular life despite problems with irritability, paranoia, anxiety, and/ or depression. There are degrees to all these symptoms. Some people can get along being a little paranoid, particularly if their loved ones understand and tolerate it. But **delusions** (thinking things that aren't real) and **hallucinations** (seeing or hearing things that aren't actually there) are more serious manifestations of prolonged stress.

CONSEQUENCES OF PTSD FOR FAMILY AND FRIENDS

Hostages and combat veterans alike have a great deal of anger, and it's usually misdirected. Vietnam war soldiers were mad at the Vietcong but in most cases, the VC were invisible, or seemed to be, and were always out of reach. Unfortunately, others were always around to catch the brunt of the soldiers' anger, and it wasn't usually fair.

Tim O'Brien, a writer and Vietnam veteran, tells the story of a soldier who was wounded in combat. Having been shot and in danger of bleeding to death, the man screamed for a medic. Unfortunately, the medic was new to combat and momentarily froze with fear. The soldier kept screaming, but the medic didn't come. Eventually—and in reality, it probably wasn't so very long—the medic reached the soldier who was by then going into shock.

The soldier recovered but suffered for a long time afterward with infections from his gun wound on his buttocks. He couldn't sit and had to apply special ointment every few hours to the wound. The soldier was temporarily moved to an office job, which at first was great, until he realized that he was no longer "one of the guys." His combat buddies had bonded with the medic, the very man who had let him go into shock.

The soldier burned with anger and kept thinking of ways to get even with the medic. All his rage was aimed at the medic, although the Vietcong were the ones who had shot him and the medic was simply a rescuer who hadn't gotten to him in time. Unable to vent his anger on the real enemy, the soldier took it out on the rescuer. This often happens with kidnapping victims. They end up more angry at those who weren't able to rescue them in time to spare them the trauma.

Children especially experience much anger after a trauma. A terrified Adam stayed in his bed during the first few seconds of the California earthquake. He was still having trouble controlling his irritability a year after the quake. He was traumatized for several reasons. First, his parents left him frightened in his room while they ran to his sister; that made him mad. Even though it was probably only a few seconds, those seconds during a trauma seem an unbearably long time. Then, after the earthquake was over, his parents moved the family all the way across the country. Adam had to leave his friends behind and start over again at a new school. His mother's attempt to protect him from further harm had resulted in more chaos. It is difficult to be mad at your parents, especially when they're trying to help. Adam let his irritability escape around others, such as new teachers and other children.

Flashbacks are frightening for everyone involved. When Paul imagined he was back in Vietnam after the neighbor's house blew up, his wife was upset and frightened. Paul was not acting like his normal self and it scared her.

Family members inevitably feel terrible for their loved ones, who are obviously in much pain. It hurts to think you can't do anything to help them. You can't take away their memories and you can't take away their shame; this is something they have to work through themselves.

A parent's greatest nightmare is losing a child. If that child is kidnapped and harmed, she blames herself for not being able to prevent it. No matter that this is unrealistic; no one can keep a child safe forever. Parents feel helpless, and in their helplessness, angry. They also feel guilty. All these feelings get jumbled up, causing a great amount of turmoil in the parent/child relationship. The child, in turn, is angry that he wasn't rescued, and probably feels guilty holding such anger toward a loved one. At this point the household becomes volatile with all the feelings of anger and helplessness.

Victims also tend to be cross with their loved ones. While relieved to be reunited with them, a part of them resents having gone through the trauma alone. As with other PTSD victims, they find it hard to trust in a relationship. Loving someone means opening yourself up to the possibility of losing him. People who have already faced death and isolation are not always willing to risk loving again. This, of course, makes it doubly hard on the loved one. He has to prove over and over again that he won't leave and that he won't stop loving.

The PTSD victim may smother the loved one with his dependence or torment her with his indifference. And he may do both at different times of the day or week. The loved one never knows what to expect or how to respond.

CHAPTER ◇ 4

Other Traumatic Situations

When I was less than two years old, I almost accidentally hanged myself in a crib. Apparently I woke up from a nap and tried to squeeze out between the bars. I succeeded in getting everything out but my head. That's when I got stuck. Having already squeezed my arms out, I couldn't pull myself back in either. I dangled there over the edge of the floor, hanging, the crib bars pressed tightly against my throat. Fortunately, I cried and when my mother heard it she ran up to see what was wrong and discovered me hanging there, turning blue.

She grabbed my dangling body and tried to push me back into the crib, but however I happened to get out, I could no longer squeeze back in. She held me up so that the bars weren't pressed against my throat, and tried to console me as the color came back to my face. The bars were made of iron, so she couldn't get me out, but at least I was able to breathe again. My mother held me like that until my uncle came home and pulled the bars apart.

I don't remember this experience myself. I've heard it repeated over the years because people marvelled that my uncle was able to bend the iron. Ironically, once people saw I was no longer choking, they believed I was over the trauma. Many people assume that young children have no memory of trauma.

According to psychologists, children under the age of twenty-eight months can't put their thoughts into words. They will feel the trauma and store memories of the feelings and sensations. Little children still react to the trauma, though. They fear trauma-related stimuli—things that remind them of the original trauma—and they reenact the traumas in their play. Most people don't notice, however, because they wouldn't expect such a youngster to recall the trauma.

Although I have no vivid memories of the episode, to this day I have an aversion to ropes, cords, and other things by which a person can hang himself. In times of stress, I can't swallow, and I feel as if I'm choking to death.

Potentially traumatic situations are all around us. Nancy Kerrigan, the figure skater who won a silver medal in the 1994 Winter Olympics, was reported to suffer with PTSD after she was clubbed. She had just finished practicing when a man jumped out of the stands and smashed her knee with a baseball bat. As far as she knew, he wanted to kill her. The television replayed scenes of her bruised and crying, whimpering, "Why me? Why me?"

In a similar fashion, Monica Seles, a tennis star, was stabbed in the back by a fanatical fan of her rival during a tennis match. We got to see the aftermath on live television. When shocking and life-threatening events happen to us, we react with the three cardinal symptoms of PTSD: hyperarousal, intrusion, and constriction. Nancy Kerrigan fortunately had therapists to help her at the Olympics, as well as increased security. Monica Seles dropped out of competitive tennis for a while—she has since returned—and has stated that she is unable to look at the scar from her wound.

Even little children are not safe from unprovoked attacks. In Stockton, California, in 1989, a gunman sprayed an elementary schoolyard with bullets, killing and injuring several children. In Tulsa, Oklahoma, in 1994, a young man marched into a Wendy's restaurant and opened fire on the teenagers gathered there for lunch. Imagine one girl's terror when the man pointed the gun at her and it misfired.

Today, people in Beirut and Bosnia expect life to be dangerous. While they've become accustomed to the shellings and unpredictability, many have also become heavy substance abusers. These people come from chronically traumatized cities, though Beirut is reportedly more normal now. Kids growing up in war zones are chronically traumatized themselves; while they may look like other kids, they are more vigilant, cautious, and anxious—suffering classic signs of PTSD.

On April 19, 1995, a 4,800-pound bomb tore apart the Federal building in downtown Oklahoma City. At first people thought international terrorists had struck the heartland of America. Later they arrested American suspects.

More than 500 people were conducting business in the Federal building that day at 9:00 A.M. One young woman stopped by to get a social security card for her four-month-old son. She brought along her son, her three-year-old daughter, her mother, and her sister, but only the woman survived the explosion.

In addition to the various government offices in the federal building, there was a day-care center on the second floor. The bomb brought seven floors down on top of the day-care center; few children survived the explosion. Across from the Federal building, glass shards from the exploding car bomb rained down on another day-care center. People as far as two blocks away were knocked over by the explosion.

One man dove under his desk when the bomb exploded. Seconds later he stuck his head out to survey the damage and realized that his desk and the floor space it occupied stood unscathed, while the rest of the floor had been blown away. He looked up at the sky and below to a gaping hole in the center of the building. He was one of the lucky ones; he got out alive. Most victims were buried in concrete and falling debris as the nine stories fell one on top of each other.

Rescue workers, as well as survivors in the building, still feel the effects of PTSD. Firefighters, mental health workers, medical doctors, and other rescue personnel from nearby cities converged on Oklahoma City to search for bodies and assist the families of the victims. At first, rescuers were buoyed by finding survivors, but as the hours wore on and bad weather hampered rescue efforts, chances of finding anyone else alive diminished. Rescue personnel were overwhelmed by such massive devastation and death. By the end of the first day, rescuers were finding more bodies than survivors. As fatigue set in, it became harder and harder to shut out their feelings. Many workers went home to their family members and wept.

As the Oklahoma City bombing has shown, the victims were not simply the people who died. The trauma greatly affected the people who survived, and especially the people who tried to rescue those buried alive. Both the survivors and the rescue personnel needed support to handle the tragedy.

Terrorist attacks on American cities are uncommon, but many neighborhoods are still dangerous to kids. Every city has its rough neighborhoods and related violence. In many places citizens are warned not to use automated teller machines at banks even in broad daylight because of the robbery risk.

One of my friends teaches at a high school in an area noted for its drive-by shootings and violence. Security personnel use metal detectors at the front doors, but guns still find their way into the school. Most students and teachers feel unsafe. My friend locks her classroom door and won't let anyone in without a pass from the front office. Students say they feel they're in a demilitarized zone when they go into the hallways: drug deals, knife fights, and guns are not uncommon.

Violence in our society has become all *too* common. Weapons such as guns are easily obtained and used for minor grievances. Kids start to get used to the violence because it surrounds them. People think that means they have adjusted, but really it serves only to harden them. If you live in an environment where people routinely get shot, and drug-crazed men and women beat up on their spouses, you come to accept that kind of behavior as normal. It makes it that much easier for you to do the same thing. Your mind and body have to go on perpetual alert from being around so much danger. You always have to watch your back. That's hyperarousal, one of the three cardinal symptoms of PTSD. Kids in these neighborhoods or housing complexes lose their sense of a future, because it's highly likely they will not live to have much of a future (another sign of PTSD). And lastly, they numb themselves to all the violence—in other words, they go through constriction, another sign of PTSD. Drugs and alcohol temporarily help kids and adults survive in this violent environment, but of course, drugs and alcohol become part of the problem.

Kids see other kinds of violent acts that they can barely comprehend. Krista was in my homeroom. In fifth grade, her grandfather died, and her mother slipped into a depression. No one knew what was wrong with Krista's mother, except that she never drove Krista to school anymore and she didn't come to any of the PTA meetings.

One morning I found my own mother exclaiming over the newspaper. Krista's mother had apparently hanged herself the day before. Krista and another sister had found her.

Krista never talked about the trauma. Her father had told her, "What's done is done. We can't change it now. I don't want to hear anymore about it." And Krista kept all that horror inside her. Years later she had turned into a sad, timid person who had left school and married at seventeen.

Sally was a recent student of mine. One evening while driving, another car crossed the center line, causing Sally to swerve, hitting yet another car and sending her soaring into the river. Her van settled upright in the river, but the water was deep and the van started to sink. Sally's son was strapped into his car seat. Carefully opening the door, she unbuckled her seatbelt and told her son to do the same. Then she hung onto the doorframe and grabbed her son. The van began sinking faster; the water began splashing into the van.

Two women had seen the accident and waded out into the river toward the quickly sinking van. Sally saw them, grabbed her son, and jumped into the river. The women reached out and grabbed Sally, who clutched her son, and they were all dragged to safety. The incredible part of this story is that Sally can't swim.

Witnessing extreme violence, even when your own life isn't in danger, is also traumatizing. People who have watched tragedies happen to others usually think, "It could have happened to me." And that's what's so scary. It *could* have happened to you. Life-threatening situations cause trauma, even when they happen to someone else. Witnessing a loved one die is even worse. Some people would prefer to be the victim. Being helpless to save a loved one from tragedy is extremely traumatic. Seeing loved ones killed or injured is more powerful than seeing strangers killed, but witnessing any act of extreme violence will provoke symptoms of PTSD.

CONSEQUENCES OF PTSD FOR THE SELF

Abraham Maslow was a psychologist who devised a "Hierarchy of Needs" to explain how people are motivated. If you think of the hierarchy as a ladder, your basic needs for survival comprise the lower rung. Those are your needs for sustaining life: eating, drinking water, and breathing. Just above those needs is the need for security or freedom from fear. Once your basic physiological needs are met, you need shelter and a safe environment. Farther up the ladder comes attachment, the need to love and be loved, and then self-esteem, the need to feel good about yourself.

The basic needs of survival, security, attachment, and self-esteem are called **deficiency needs** because Maslow considered a person deficient or missing something without any one of them. A person would not be motivated to move on to his **growth needs**, things that improve his character and mind, until he had satisfied these primary needs. The growth needs are: cognitive (the need to learn new things, not just school subjects); aesthetic (the need for beauty in your environment); self-actualization (living up to one's potential); and transcendence (spiritual needs).

Let's look at the lower part of Maslow's ladder. If one lives in a violent environment, he is stuck trying to meet his need for security. He is not motivated to decorate his apartment with fancy paintings (aesthetic needs) or take up meditation (transcendence) just yet. He's concerned about making ends meet or keeping himself from getting shot on the way to the store. Now, think about your average student in a rundown neighborhood, beseiged by gang violence. This kid has to walk home every day through a war zone. Is he going to be a good student? According to Maslow, how could he when his most pressing need is to stay alive (security needs) rather than learn algebra (cognitive needs)? In other words, when schools and neighborhoods are dangerous places, not much learning is going to occur. People become chronically stressed and do not think beyond their immediate future (getting home safely that day).

The victim is constantly on the alert, and that takes a toll on his good humor as well as his body. Traumatized people, especially chronically traumatized people, often look much older than others their age. Chronic anxiety wears a body out.

Victims become edgy and irritable over seemingly inconsequential things. They may blow up if you forget to return a pencil you borrowed. They may think you're laughing at them if you smile as they walk by. These are symptoms of paranoia and are part of their hyperarousal.

Continually faced with bad memories, victims often get depressed, especially if they can't reconcile the memories or make them go away. Depression causes a person to cry a lot, to lose hope that she'll ever get better, to lose sleep, her appetite, and her interest in her appearance. Victims of violence are often afraid to go to sleep—to fall asleep, one has to relax. Chronically stressed people and those who have witnessed extreme acts of violence are not initially capable of relaxing. Insomnia—not being able to get a good night's sleep—only compounds the problem, because sleep deprivation takes away a person's good judgment and makes him that much more irritable. If someone lives in a frightening environment, it may not be safe to sleep. That person either has to numb himself to the constant threats or live in terror.

A constricted life is filled with losses. If you have to avoid certain people, you become lonely when they are the only ones around. If you are afraid to venture out, you may miss out on many community events. If you can't let yourself love anyone because she might take her life one day, you've lost the chance to share your life with someone.

Sally, my student, still has nightmares about plunging into the river. Of course, in her nightmares, she doesn't always escape or she leaves behind her son. During the day, Sally tries not to think about her trauma. Even though the van was pulled out of the river and salvaged, she refuses to drive it. Furthermore, she won't ride in a car anywhere near that particular river.

If Sally is angry, which occurs because the accident wasn't her fault, she directs the anger toward herself. Her classmates have described her as timid and passive; her eventual reliving of the trauma (especially her heroism) was surprising to those who knew her. In the first few weeks of class, Sally was psychologically numb. She didn't even know how she felt about the whole experience. Once she started talking about it and got in touch with her panic and anger, she uncovered a wealth of other things she liked about herself.

Initially, the numbing had helped her keep functioning day to day. "If I thought about how close we'd come to dying," she told me, "I would have gone crazy." The problem was—and always is—it takes an awful lot of energy to "not think about things." It is better to accept the pain and put all that energy to more positive use.

Little children cannot recall their traumas in words, but most grow up fearing and avoiding things that remind them of their traumas. But they probably do these things unconsciously, never completely understanding why they do what they do. I have never allowed my kids to play on their beds with toys that have long cords or even string. While I knew I was afraid they'd get tangled up in these cords in the night, I was not consciously associating their choking with mine forty years ago.

CONSEQUENCES OF PTSD FOR FAMILY AND FRIENDS

Chronically vigilant people can make mistakes. Sometimes being so alert to possible danger makes you see danger where none exists. Sometimes people overreact in traffic because they assume other people mean to cut them off. Easily provoked people tend to turn off other people.

Family members and friends may make belated attempts to shield you from further danger, but most victims don't want to be overprotected. People expect others to keep them from harm (which isn't entirely possible), and yet people want to go off and do their own thing when the mood strikes. You can't have it both ways. So, victims develop overdependence on loved ones and resent them at the same time.

Some people lose their ability to form attachments; it's simply not worth the effort. Loving is too scary. Many victims of violence prefer to look out for themselves. They may seem friendly at times, but feel they can't afford to love.

Constricted people sometimes restrict not only their own lives but everyone else's as well. Residents of rough neighborhoods try to keep their children safe by locking them inside. The adult victims still don't feel safe, and their children feel punished for living in an unsafe environment.

Victims also stop trusting people. They believe the world is not a safe place. Cars can go into rivers, mothers hang themselves, and terrorists kill innocent people. As a result of seeing danger everywhere, victims distrust everyone. Friends and relatives probably understand where this distrust comes from but can get tired of the victim's ever-present fear. And accommodating his or her wishes to avoid places or people may cause friction after a while.

TREATMENT
FOR PTSD

CHAPTER 5

Negative Ways of Coping

Anyone who has ever suffered a traumatic experience has probably found himself using some or all of these methods to keep the memories at bay. He has also probably found that these methods don't work for long, simply creating more problems in the end.

ALCOHOL AND DRUGS

Alcohol seems to be a good way to numb emotions. You may feel frightened or anxious so you decide to have a beer or two, and then before you know it, you're not thinking about that problem anymore. If memories stayed away for good and alcohol didn't lead to so many other physical problems, this might be a suitable remedy. But traumatic memories are not dulled by alcohol. Under the influence you might not feel their impact, but the memories are still there and will continue to haunt you. Furthermore, you'll have to keep drinking more to keep them quiet.

Contrary to what most people think, alcohol is a depressant, not a stimulant. That means it brings you down; it does not give you energy. Feelings sometimes become exaggerated when combined with alcohol, even as they sometimes seem less significant. You cannot always predict which will happen to you. Some people become moody and depressed; others act silly and inappropriate.

Alcohol abuse also ravages your body. It destroys your liver and can lead to heart complications and addiction. Alcohol abuse ruins families as well. When people depend on alcohol to banish their problems, they often retreat from others. They can also turn mean and uncooperative because alcohol destroys judgment. A person who has had too much to drink lacks the coordination or reflex time to drive a car safely. He also lacks the good sense to know when he's out of line and inappropriate. Children are afraid of unpredictable adults; adults are afraid of their youngsters who are unreachable because of alcohol.

If poor health and ruined relationships are not enough to turn you off to alcohol, consider this: alcohol disturbs sleep. Many victims of PTSD are plagued with insomnia and nightmares. Alcohol may relax them enough initially to fall asleep, but their sleep will be light and fragmented. Alcoholics sleep fitfully; they wake up a lot and then have trouble falling back asleep. The nightmares don't necessarily go away, either. And predictably, when someone quits drinking, she has an onslaught of nightmares for the first several nights.

Drugs function much the same way. Some may pep you up so that you feel good, but you come back down eventually, and the memories will still be there. Others claim to relax you and mellow you out. If that's all that happened, they might be a good alternative to facing your trauma.

But that's not all that happens. Depending on what drugs you use and how much, you can ruin your health, your initiative, your relationships, and your brain. Drugs can impair judgment because they disrupt chemical messages in the brain and provoke violent mood swings. Drugs, even prescription drugs, can disrupt sleep patterns, causing insomnia or loss of dream sleep. If all your dreams have been nightmares, you might think that's a good thing. However, a loss of REM sleep—during which dreaming usually occurs—is detrimental to your mental health. REM sleep seems to refresh the mind so that you are able to think more clearly in the morning. Without sufficient REM sleep, your judgment is not as sharp and your mood isn't as stable.

Since drugs can be an escape, it's easy to become addicted—especially to the less expensive, quicker-acting highs. Drugs can also lead to physical problems including heart attacks and overdoses. They are also very costly.

SEXUAL ACTING OUT

Some psychologists view sexual acting out as an escape, but most believe it is a reenactment of the original trauma. People who use their bodies promiscuously have usually been victims of chronic sexual abuse. They either decide that they are "damaged goods" already and promiscuity does not matter, or they end up reliving what once happened to them.

Adele was sexually abused by her stepfather from the age of five. By the time she was in high school, she had earned a reputation for being "fast and easy" with the guys. Although Adele was ashamed of her promiscuity, she couldn't bring herself to stop this pattern of behavior. She had learned at an early age that people related to her in a sexual way, and that was the only way she knew of making and keeping friends.

Eventually Adele ended up in therapy for severe depression. Within a few sessions, she found herself propositioning her male therapist. Even though she needed this man to relate to her on a more professional level, she couldn't help but try to sexualize this relationship as well. Fortunately, her therapist recognized this behavior as a trauma reenactment and maintained the strict boundaries of their relationship.

Other victims become so disgusted with themselves that they no longer care what happens to them. Having no belief in a future, they persist in behavior that might bring them physical satisfaction (initially) or financial gain, but ultimately confirms their low opinion of themselves.

At the same time, sexual acting out is an escape. You can't dwell on scary memories when you are out supposedly having a good time. But the problem remains: your self-esteem suffers when you realize you haven't gotten rid of the memories (except temporarily) and you've risked disease.

Some trauma victims resort to sex as a way to reassure themselves that they're still desirable. But being desirable and undoing the trauma are two different things. One rape victim agonized over whether to report her boyfriend for date rape. She finally decided not to press charges because "no one would have believed her," and she didn't want to be "raped" again by the judicial system. She was still enraged, though, and dreamed of getting back at the guy for having taken her against her will.

Ironically, she became very promiscuous on campus, with many men except this old boyfriend, apparently as a way to prove she wasn't a victim. Her sexual acting out was a way of revenge, although to others it appeared a reenactment of the original trauma. And it solved nothing.

BEHAVIORAL PROBLEMS IN SCHOOL

Some people purposely get in trouble in school because it takes their minds off the original trauma. If you get detention for disrupting the class, chances are that everyone's going to focus on your classroom antics, not what might have been happening at home. In this sense, behavioral problems are an escape but can compound your problems.

Some kids feel so out of control that it just naturally extends to their time in school. Adam, the boy who survived the earthquake, might fit into this category. He was traumatized by the earthquake (over which he had no control), then shook up by his move across country (over which he had no control), and finally upset by the move from his rental house to his newly built house. Is it any wonder he had trouble controlling his behavior in school? The trauma had to manifest itself somehow.

Some kids have trouble with authority figures because they find it's too frightening to take their real anger out on their parents. Some people let their grades slide because they don't see much of a future for themselves anyway or it's a way to get back at their parents. Either way, acting out is a way to escape thinking about what is *really* upsetting them and to let go of a little anger.

Acting out does not help relieve the original trauma, nor does it endear you to the authority figures. You end up with more things to feel angry, guilty, and sorry about.

SUICIDAL THOUGHTS

A sense of not having a future is part of PTSD. People who no longer care about life may behave recklessly and get killed. One Vietnam veteran began sky-diving after his stint in Vietnam. He wasn't purposely taking up a sport that would kill him, but he was putting himself at risk every time he jumped out of a plane. The thrill of doing something so dangerous took his mind off his memories of Vietnam—for a while.

Other victims of PTSD may be more direct, purposely setting out to kill themselves. This is a way to end the suffering from the trauma. The problem with suicide is that you hurt others in addition to yourself. If you succeed in taking your life, you will have traumatized those you left behind. Remember Krista: not only did Krista's mother leave the family by hanging herself, but she horrified the family when they found her dead. The mother may have escaped her depression, but she passed an even greater horror onto her children.

Suicides don't always succeed. Many victims botch their attempts and in so doing develop other physical problems. Drug overdoses are not always fatal but can ruin your internal organs so that your body deteriorates well before you die. Sometimes you damage your brain so sufficiently that you can't function anymore, and you're left without the energy or ability to carry out another suicide attempt.

Some victims don't mean to kill themselves. People who have numbed themselves in the past to a great trauma find it hard to retrieve their feelings later. They resort to cutting themselves, watching their wounds bleed, and trying to recapture the feeling of pain. Unfortunately, they are liable to do some real damage in an effort to reexperience pain.

People who attempt suicide may do so because they're tired but can't sleep long enough or deeply enough to benefit them. They don't necessarily mean to die; they just want an escape from their problems and their intrusive memories. Often, they are not thinking rationally because their hope is to reunite with a deceased loved one, or they want to punish others with their death, as if they'll be able to watch these people tormented at their funerals. Suicide is not the ultimate revenge because you don't live to see the results. Dying is not a way to cope with bad memories.

LOSING YOUR FEELINGS

Tony had been sexually abused by his uncle. By age thirty-five Tony had experienced a few homosexual affairs but had no steady relationships. While he probably was once attractive, he had lost interest in his appearance. He was also hard to reach. Tony had repressed his feelings for so long that he no longer looked angry when he talked about things that made him angry and he didn't smile when he was pleased with something. Essentially, he didn't feel emotions anymore. In sessions when we talked about his earlier abuse, he could not seem to connect his words to any genuine feelings.

Tony still lived with his aging parents and was afraid to cause a disturbance by telling them what had happened so long ago. But the injustice of it all drove him crazy. To live with himself, and the people who had failed to protect him, he had to contain his feelings. He dissociated every time his parents went to the movies because that is when the uncle had fondled him. He got so good at "going away in his head" that he could endure the sexual humiliation and excitement, which was all rolled into one, without comment. Eventually, whenever anything scary happened or he got angry, he went away in his mind. By the time he sought therapy, he didn't have to dissociate anymore; his feelings—all feelings—were gone.

Tony couldn't maintain any relationships and people were uncomfortable around him. He never looked happy or excited and he didn't know how to get angry. He was, in a word, emotionless.

Numbness does serve a purpose to the victim of a trauma. Initially, it allows him to go on functioning in the face of extreme terror. When a person is better able to cope, and often this takes time, his numbness gives way to anger. Anger is a great energizer and gets the victim moving again. But some people get stuck in the numb stage. They don't want to feel the pain and horror all over again, so they keep their feelings under wraps. You can not selectively feel the good stuff and deny the bad. Emotionless people go through life isolated from others and unable to integrate the trauma into their life experience. More important, they miss out on joyful events that come along.

AVOIDANCE OF REMINDERS

In the short term, avoiding reminders of a trauma helps make the memories and feelings tolerable. Sally stayed away from Riverside Drive and didn't have to deal with the trauma of seeing the scene of her accident. After a while, however, it became harder and harder to avoid reminders. Sally missed the festivals they held down on the riverbank, as well as the road races and activities they have there every year.

In the long run, the victim is using avoidance to escape working out her feelings about the trauma. Memories don't die simply because you're not tapping into them. Eventually they will come back when a new reminder brings them to the surface. In the meantime, you're missing out on things by restricting your life. When you live in fear, even of a memory, you are surrendering to the power of the trauma. There are far better ways to deal with your feelings.

Repressed memories don't go away; they're alive and well inside us. Until you confront the trauma and your feelings surrounding it, you'll be subject to repetitive dreams and reenactments, which could set you up for even more abuse.

CHILDREN'S REACTIONS TO TRAUMA

Children sometimes react to trauma through **rigidity** and **regression**. Rigidity is a form of avoidance. The child has been so shocked by the event or series of events that he withdraws into himself or his home. He may not want to go outside anymore or to visit a friend's house. Constricting his life in such a rigid fashion (which isn't necessarily a conscious act) is a normal reaction to trauma, but if it continues for a long time, it's a negative way of coping. Rigid children grow up to be rigid adults whose emotions are deadened, as in the example of Tony.

Children and teenagers tend to regress in times of stress. That means they revert to behavior more suited to a younger child. If they're traumatized when they're six, they may regress to acting like a three-year-old. Any time before the trauma was a safer time, and the child can reduce his anxiety by acting as if he's back in that safer time. Of course, regression doesn't change anything. You can act younger but you really don't become younger, and

the experiences don't go away. Regression is normal behavior for anyone overwhelmed by trauma, but if it per-
sists too long, it becomes another avoidance.

Finally, although it might be normal to try to make
some sense out of the trauma, there comes a time when
you have to move on. You cannot make sense out of
something senseless. Bad things happen in this world.
People can drive themselves crazy trying to understand
why the awful event happened to them, but usually no
rational explanation exists. Spending all of your time figur-
ing out the greater meaning of the event will take time
away from your healing.

CHAPTER ◇ 6

A Support System

Most important to a trauma victim is the knowledge that he or she is safe. He can't work on other issues such as anger and sorrow at losses until he is certain his immediate environment is secure. His loved ones and friends, and to some extent, the community, can provide that support.

YOUR LOVED ONES

A woman was jogging through a park some time ago. For a short stretch, the trail ran alongside a heavily traveled street. As she jogged along this stretch, she saw a carload of men pass by. She thought the car backfired, and then she stumbled. As she tried to regain her footing, she saw the blood on her thigh and realized she'd been shot.

Her boyfriend found her and rushed her to the hospital. Fortunately the wound was not life-threatening, but the woman was severely traumatized. Now when she jogs, her boyfriend stays at her side or she goes in a group. Her boyfriend's continuing concern for her safety made her feel less traumatized. She was also relieved to see that park officials also responded quickly. They increased lighting, planted more bushes to separate the trail from the street, and added security.

When a person has suffered a trauma, she feels frightened and alone. Loved ones can do two things for her. They can reassure her of their continuing love at a time when she might not be feeling so lovable, and they can stay with her to keep her safe.

If the victim has been raped, she will feel safer if someone she knows and trusts accompanies her to the hospital and police station. The exam and police questioning could seem like another violation.

However, the loved one is not helpful to the victim when he or she overreacts to the situation. You don't help the victim feel safe again by taking away her independence. If the loved one expresses all the victim's rage for her, the victim doesn't learn to express the rage herself. If the loved one restricts the victim's life, the victim never learns to conquer her fears. That's what happened to Janet.

Following the rapes of Janet's friends, her parents drove to the house. They ordered Janet to come home, but Janet thought it was more important that she stay, no matter how scary that was. Janet spent that next night with her landlord's family in order to feel safe and to appease her parents. As soon as her landlord had installed more locks and bright lights around her house, Janet moved back to conquer her fears. She developed close ties to the area police, who came by frequently to make sure she was safe.

After a disaster, loved ones can help by removing victims to safer areas. However, it's important to let the victim make these decisions. He or she needs to be able to decide when to go back and face the fears. Loved ones need to protect, but not constrict.

Trauma victims especially need their loved ones to listen to them and believe them. Rape and abuse victims often feel guilt over the trauma, as if they had some control over the event. Of course, people don't deserve their traumas; these are terrible things that sometimes just happen. The victim needs to talk about the experience to sort out his or her feelings. Some loved ones are so caught up in their own anguish because they couldn't prevent the trauma that they can't stand to hear the victim's pain.

But that's another thing the victim needs from a loved one: to listen without censoring feelings. The victim doesn't need to be judged. He or she doesn't need to be told, "Oh, don't think about that anymore." The feelings don't go away simply because the victim stops talking about them. And crying is not a bad reaction to a trauma. Crying is a normal response to a loss, and any trauma victim has suffered a loss, whether it's virginity, possessions, or a sense of innocence. If the victim has no one with whom to share feelings, he or she is likely to bottle them up. Feelings and traumatic memories have a way of surfacing in dreams and flashbacks.

On the other hand, if the trauma victim can tell friends how lonely, scared, or ashamed she feels, and the friend continues to care, she will start to feel safe and lovable once again.

SEXUAL ISSUES

A person who has been sexually assaulted needs special care from his or her partner. Any subsequent act of lovemaking will be a remainder of the assault, so the loved one has to be very careful not to pressure the victim to have sex.

One young woman's husband was understandably enraged about her rape. However, he was more wrapped up in his own rage than he was in hers. After the rape, he forced her into having sex, claiming he wanted to erase the image of the man with her. Needless to say, this second "rape" compounded the original trauma.

Abstaining from sex in a married relationship requires an understanding, loving partner. This person knows how traumatic the experience has been for the victim and recognizes how traumatic sex will probably seem again. He therefore lets the victim make the decision as to when to resume this aspect of their relationship.

HONESTY

Friends and relatives need to be honest when dealing with a trauma victim, especially when the victim's behavior is inappropriate. Often victims are so wrapped up in their pain that they don't recognize when their anger is irrational or directed at the wrong person.

One combat veteran, John, became frustrated with his realtor's efforts to sell his house. In a rage one day, he called the realtor and threatened to blow up the house. Apparently the realtor believed John might make good on his threat, so he called John's wife. She in turn called a therapist, who confronted John about his inappropriate behavior. It's one thing to tell someone you're mad at him; it's quite another to threaten him. Besides, a lot of John's anger stemmed from his wartime experiences, not this realtor.

Children especially need to know someone is concerned enough to set limits on their behavior. After a traumatic experience, they may feel out of control. If they cannot bring themselves under control, they need a loving adult to do it for them. Setting limits and pointing out unacceptable behavior are gestures of people who care.

If your uncle, a combat veteran, gets upset when bills come due and starts ranting and raving, it's okay to tell him he's scaring you. Ranting and raving around others is not appropriate behavior; he needs to hear this. After all, the victim's goal is to heal from his trauma and reconnect with others. He won't be able to reconnect if he's scaring people off.

ABUSE ISSUES

A child abuse victim will recover more quickly if he or she has a support system. Ideally, his parents are that support, but what if the perpetrator is the parent? In such cases it is vital that a loved one believe the victim's story. If the nonabusing parent doesn't believe the child and the perpetrator is still around, the child remains in danger. The perpetrator needs to be removed from the home to guarantee the child's safety. That doesn't mean the nonabusing parent must divorce the perpetrator, but he or she must see that the perpetrator receives treatment. Relying on the perpetrator's promise to change sets the child up for further trauma.

Ironically, when the police step in, they usually remove the victim from the abusive home. This is meant to reassure the child, but more often than not it convinces the child that he or she did something wrong because the child is the one being punished. The victim is the one who is isolated from family.

Family members must consider that the child is telling the truth. Sexual abuse is not something children easily talk about. They typically feel responsible for the adult's behavior, and as a result, ashamed and soiled. It is with tremendous reluctance that children bring these stories to their parents. If the family member immediately discounts the story and doesn't bother to look into it, the victim has nowhere else to go. The victim may think no one will believe her and that she is not safe anywhere.

If the perpetrator is another relative, the victim's parents must act in the child's best interests, even when that means confronting the relative. The victim first needs his parents to put a stop to the abuse. Ensuring the victim's safety means never leaving the victim alone with the relative. Usually it means getting the relative out of the house.

Many years ago our friends' five-year-old son was molested by his great-uncle. When his parents found out that the uncle had been fondling the boy at a family get-together, they were enraged. The father wanted to press charges, but the uncle's family talked them out of it. The wife's mother said, "We'll see that it doesn't happen again. If you press charges, then everyone will know and then think how the boy will feel. Just drop the whole thing and let it stay in the family."

The boy's parents agreed, but they didn't feel good about it. They never left the boy alone with his uncle, but their anger didn't subside: the boy had been abused, but nothing legal had happened to the perpetrator.

The parents had responded supportively by believing the child and taking steps to ensure his safety. But the uncle's family had not been supportive by wanting to keep the abuse a secret. Keeping secrets makes the victim continue to feel dirty and ashamed. People who abuse children need more help than their families can give them. Helping to keep their secrets allows them to continue doing what they've been doing. Loved ones don't necessarily have to press charges to ensure that the abuse will stop, but they do need to force the abuser to get treatment. Sometimes pressing charges is the only way to force the perpetrator into treatment.

A SUPPORTIVE COMMUNITY

A supportive community, including neighbors, police, helping professionals, and the media, reaffirms the victim's experiences. It says, "Yes, you are right to feel outraged. What happened to you was terrible, and your well-being matters to us."

That's why the Vietnam Memorial in Washington, DC, is so important. When soldiers returned from the Vietnam war, there were no parades or yellow ribbons in honor of their service. More often than not, soldiers left the battlefields, hopped on a commercial airliner, and arrived home alone without fanfare. They didn't come back as troops. Many were berated for being soldiers, even though they had been drafted.

As you may recall from the Persian Gulf War, soldiers returned to great acclaim. This happened after World Wars I and II as well. A grateful nation couldn't take away the soldiers' horrible experiences, but it could make them feel that they had endured terror for the greater good. There was no gratitude for the returning Vietnam veterans, which made their wartime experiences that much harder to bear. Sometimes it seemed like the only people to understand their traumas were other veterans. When the Vietnam Memorial was erected many years later to honor the soldiers who had died in battle or were missing in action, Vietnam veterans at last had something that paid tribute to their service. By supporting the memorial, people were telling these veterans that Vietnam war soldiers had an important place in history, too.

A former Miss America came forward with the story that she had been sexually abused for years by her father, a wealthy philanthropist. She wasn't sure her community would believe her, but when her sisters followed with reports of similar abuses, it was too much to discount. Other victims of incest rallied around this woman, greatly relieved that someone would be a spokesperson for them. When someone is willing to enlighten the community at great expense to her reputation, she deserves recognition. It is to educate the community that Janet suggested I use her real name here. "When the community sees how often these crimes happen to good people, sexual assault will not be such a deep, dark secret. Good people have to speak out and say, 'this happened to me.'"

When Polly Klaus was kidnapped in California, her community banded together to search for her, to post signs in other towns, and to staff hotlines. Hollywood actress Winona Ryder put up money as a reward leading to Polly's safe return. And the community support didn't end when Polly died. Citizens lobbied statewide for stiffer penalties for repeat offenders. (Polly's abductor had committed other felonies in the past.) While the community support couldn't bring Polly back to her parents, it must have made the loss somewhat easier to bear. The community shared in the pain, making the parents' trauma a shared experience.

When disasters strike, whole communities rally around the victims. The Red Cross erected tent cities for the many Floridians made homeless by Hurricane Andrew while other organizations and states sent food, supplies, and volunteers. When the floods of 1993 ruined crops and buried towns, supportive people were back at the post offices with more boxes of food and supplies. Expressions of goodwill and concrete support make the trauma victims feel appreciated, not scorned.

The media can also be supportive; after all, they reflect the community at large. By bringing the subjects of physical and sexual abuse out into the open, they allow victims to regain their dignity. People often don't think about abuse until it happens to someone they know or somebody famous. When someone as well known and wealthy as former football star O. J. Simpson was accused of killing his wife, it's easier to believe that anyone could commit a similar act. Once society recognizes the extent of the problem, it is more likely to do something about it. Because of the court trial of O. J. Simpson, people now know that physical abuse happens in even the most lavish homes.

The media still have to go further in educating people about sexual abuse. Many people still assume a that boy can't be raped (if he gets an erection, it must mean he was sexually aroused). Boys, and men as well, get erections when stimulated; it does not mean they *enjoy* or have consented to being fondled or penetrated. A supportive community doesn't condemn its victims, no matter which gender they happen to be.

Likewise, the judicial system need not censure the victim, though that happens more often than not. In 1972, when Janet and her friends faced their rapist in court, the courts were not as sensitive to rape victims. The defense attorney tried to paint a picture of three unsupervised cocktail waitresses crying rape. The assailant's father came over and leered at Janet, telling her that it couldn't possibly have been his son. The women felt attacked on all counts; the police challenged their stories right from the start, though they admitted later that they would have put Janet and her friends on the stand if only they thought they could hold up under intense cross-examination. The neighbors speculated about the women, and the defense attorney made it his job to question everything the victims said about the rapist (who was eventually convicted).

Today police and hospital workers are trained to deal with rape victims with much more sensitivity. First, victims need to feel safe; if the courts and the community do not respond supportively by locking up the rapists or taking steps to protect public areas, the victim no longer feels safe. How can he or she heal?

A supportive community believes that "bad things happen to good people," not that "people get what they deserve." The world is an unpredictable place, and bad things happen all the time. Although we cannot always prevent or foresee the traumatic event, we can survive it and respond supportively so others will survive too. Trauma victims still have to work through their experiences by themselves, but those who have the support of their loved ones and community will survive the traumas best.

CHAPTER 7

Positive Ways to Deal with PTSD

T rying to escape the pain of a trauma doesn't usually work. The only positive way to deal with your experience is to confront it. Facing the pain is intended to empower you. You're not empowered when you're running away from your fears.

After a disaster such as a fire, flood, or tornado, teams of professionals usually arrive at the site to help survivors cope with the trauma. These support groups tend to be minimarathon sessions at first, where victims can talk out their feelings with others who have gone through the experience. The groups are helpful for two reasons: they get the victims and survivors talking and not burying their pain, and they help victims and survivors bond with others who have also survived the disaster.

What's initially scary about a disaster is that the victim feels so alone. Support groups get the victims and survivors together and help them sort out how they feel. Groups have a greater capacity to bear pain than any one individual. Survivors can scream and cry without fearing that their pain is too much for one therapist to handle. There is also an instant camaraderie between people who have been through a trauma. Sharing pain helps to lessen it.

Hospitals and mental health centers are quick to respond to community tragedies as well. When the man shot up the Wendy's fast-food restaurant in Tulsa, Oklahoma, a local psychiatric clinic and hospital sent trained workers, including social workers and psychologists, to area schools to help the students cope with the trauma. (Many students had been in the restaurant or its parking lot at the time of the shooting.) Having crisis intervention workers report to the schools increases the number of victims and survivors reached. Many people are skeptical of outside groups offering free counseling, but when the counselors are in the schools, they are no longer considered "outside."

EDUCATION

Not everyone who has been traumatized is in need of psychotherapy. Sometimes, it is enough to give the survivor time to calm down and then advise him or her what symptoms he or she might experience in the future. If a person knows, for example, that he's likely to have nightmares for a while, he may not fear them so much.

Everyone dreams, although we aren't sure just why we dream. Some say we dream to unwind from the previous day's accumulation of stress. Others say that the brain is constantly firing and receiving messages, and creates a story to go along with these random firings. Whatever the reason, whenever people have suffered a tragedy, they dream specifically about that tragedy, usually devising different endings to the story.

Victims and survivors need to know that frightening dreams, especially those that blame them for the trauma, are normal. Most victims believe they were to blame, even though they probably weren't. Unfortunately, what some people are afraid to say out loud comes forth in their dreams. Often what you think about the trauma comes out of the mouths of the people in your dreams.

Trauma victims also have dreams in which they die. Dreaming about your death does not forecast your death. It is a very normal experience for people who have had something very traumatic happen to them. Some people think they'll die of a heart attack if they dream they're falling and then hit the pavement. They think it's too shocking for the body to visualize its own death. But frequently victims do dream about their deaths or see themselves dead, and they live to tell about it.

Victims will also be angry, paranoid, and numb at times, sometimes swinging wildly back and forth between these emotions. A friend named Shawna was divorced several years ago; the divorce proceedings were hostile, and at one point her husband had threatened to kill her. Shawna went through periods of extreme anger. She wanted help in slashing her ex-husband's tires when she found his car outside his girlfriend's house. She spent hours thinking up plans to embarrass him publicly. After a week or two of rage, she'd cycle into apathy. A week later, she would hear "their song" on the radio and start sliding into a depression. Weeks of sadness and longing to get back at her ex-husband would follow before she'd be asking for help again in slashing his tires.

It would be easier if the bad feelings came all at once and then went away for good, but that doesn't happen. If you realize that you'll have good days interspersed with bad days, you will be less likely to succumb the first time a good day turns bad. It's just part of the healing process.

ONGOING SUPPORT GROUPS

Support groups are lifelines for rape victims and combat veterans. People who have survived these traumas usually staff the groups, and therefore are well aware of how the victim may be feeling. A rape victim may think he or she is the only one ever to have felt so afraid or angry; it's comforting not only to know that others have been through these very same feelings, but that they have survived them. Seeing people farther along the path to recovery is an encouragement to persevere.

Combat veterans do well in veteran support groups. They heal more quickly in the company of others who have been through similar experiences. If you think you're the only one in the world who has committed an atrocity, you'll appreciate hearing someone else's confession. You will realize that you're not really so awful, or that you're not alone in your envisioned "awfulness."

Groups can be daunting with so much emotion clustered in one place. If you're too immersed in your own pain, you might try some individual work until you're ready for a group.

As mentioned earlier, groups are able to bear a lot of pain, but they also stir up a lot of pain for others who may not yet be able to tolerate it. You can learn how others managed their pain, and find out some tips for surviving "the system," but if you're newly traumatized, the depth of feeling may be too much for you at this time.

THERAPY

Therapy exists in several different forms. You can be seen by yourself in individual therapy, with your spouse in couples therapy, or with the rest of your family in family therapy. Different traumas respond to different therapeutic approaches. If a tragedy affected the whole family and now one child is acting out, the whole family should be treated. It's hard to change the system (the whole family) when only one part (the person with the problem) comes in for help. If all the members of the family are treated together, they can all adjust to the changes that the "identified patient" needs to make.

The only exception is sexual abuse. For the most part, abused children are not treated with their victimizing relative. It's just too threatening at first. Abuse victims are treated individually, with the nonabusing parent, or in a group of similarly abused peers. (Therapy is discussed further in the following chapter.)

MEDICATION

For single event traumas, medication usually is not recommended. Anti-anxiety medications, such as Valium, are not very helpful in the long run, and they can easily be abused. These pills offer a temporary respite from anxiety, but they do nothing to erase the trauma. More significantly, they quickly become a crutch.

Better choices are **beta-blocking agents**, which are medications used to treat physical signs of stress such as heart palpitations, sweating, and shaky knees. If you have to confront frightening situations where you've suffered a trauma in the past, these medications may help desensitize you to a particular fear. You take them fifteen minutes or so before you're likely to encounter the source of your fears. With your physical symptoms of fear under control, you're better able to manage your emotional fears.

If, for example, you were attacked by a rabid dog running loose in your neighborhood, you would no doubt be traumatized both by the dog and by the painful shots you had to take. Later, you might have trouble walking past the house of the people who have two German shepherds that bark menacingly from behind their fence. If you have to walk past this house to get to school, you're going to have to master your fear. The beta-blocking agents prescribed by your doctor will help get you started. They'll manage your physical symptoms; you'll handle your fears. After a while, you can manage without them.

ANTIDEPRESSANTS

Antidepressants are helpful if your post-traumatic stress symptoms are complicated by grief. Antidepressants work by allowing more of a brain chemical—serotonin or norepinephrine—to remain circulating in your brain. For reasons not clearly known to scientists, a decline in these chemicals precipitates or exacerbates a depression. Trauma can alter brain chemistry. Antidepressants also alter brain chemistry and by doing so affect mood. Long-term psychotherapy may help ease a depression, but medication will speed recovery.

Bear in mind that there are no pills to get rid of anger. The person who has been through a trauma has to come to terms with the rage and sense of injustice. You succeed in doing this only when you examine your feelings and work your way through the grief process.

Therapy can last from a few sessions (crisis management) to years. The next chapter discusses what happens during treatment. Trauma reactions are never permanently resolved. You may think you've recovered, but you may reexperience all your old feelings when you encounter another stressful point in your life such as a marriage, the birth of a child, or a child reaching a certain age. That does not mean you never resolved your crisis; it simply means that a new crisis has reopened old wounds. A brief return to therapy can help remedy the problems.

SUMMARY

Educate your family and friends about your symptoms and treatment. The more they know and understand your situation, the more supportive they can be. Don't make a secret of your trauma. You don't have to take out ads in the Sunday paper, but you should not behave as if you had done something dirty or shameful. Bad things happen; that's a fact of life.

Let your family and friends know what you need. If you feel like talking, find someone who will listen. Don't assume that "father knows best" when he tells you not to think about such things. Talking is a release. You also help others to see that PTSD is a very real condition. If you have been assaulted on the way to your car, you're going to have a lot of anxiety about walking to your car after dark in the future. Don't try to make light of your feelings. Your terror is understandable and very real. Most people in your situation would feel the same adrenalin surge when alone on a dark street at night.

PTSD is not overcome by thinking of other things. Survivors of trauma have to work hard to confront and overcome fears. Don't pretend that it's no big deal. It's hard work, and you have a right to be proud of yourself for taking the steps to heal.

Nonetheless, you can let go of the scary feelings when you need a break. The fact that you are not trying to bury your feelings doesn't mean you have to think about them all the time. It's okay to put them aside every so often, as long as you are consciously putting them aside. Suppressing is different from repressing or pretending the memories are not there. When you suppress, you know the memories are still there until you're ready to confront them again.

Above all, be kind to yourself. Eat well, get plenty of sleep (or rest, if sleep is hard to come by), and spend time with people who can offer comfort to you.

CHAPTER 8

Choosing the Right Therapist

ome practical matters help decide which therapist is right for you. Therapists, whether social workers, psychologists, or psychiatrists, charge from $75 an hour and up, so most people need to rely on their health insurance to pay the bill.

When you use your insurance coverage, you have to go along with what the professional insurance company says it will cover. Most places have their own clinicians on staff or several in the community to whom they refer. Today, the emphasis is on short-term psychotherapy, usually crisis resolution. Your insurance company will probably pay for 80 percent of your treatment if you see someone it recommends and you do not exceed the number of sessions covered. Some policies cover 100 percent of the time-limited sessions.

If you don't have insurance, or don't choose to use it, then you pay either the full cost of treatment or on a sliding scale. Some therapists charge what you can afford to pay, but you should check that out ahead of time. If you can't find someone you can afford, check out the mental-health centers in your community. You can find these places in the yellow pages of your phone book under "mental health." They offer a variety of low-cost services, but there is usually a waiting list.

Another problem is that when you rely on insurance coverage, your insurer has the right to know your diagnosis and treatment goals. If you or your parents can afford it, you might prefer paying for therapy out of pocket for privacy reasons.

CREDENTIALS

It doesn't really matter what type of professional you choose. A clinical social worker has received his Master's degree or Ph.D. in social work and then specialized in clinical (counseling) work. If he or she is licensed, a clinical social worker will have passed a rigorous national exam and worked for at least two years under supervision of another licensed clinical social worker. Many social workers specialize and provide the bulk of the counseling at mental-health agencies.

A clinical psychologist has probably received a Ph.D. in clinical psychology and passed a rigorous national exam, too, if he or she is licensed. The clinical psychologist specializes in counseling. Other psychologists specialize in research or school counseling. An advantage to psychologists is that they can administer tests if necessary and interpret the results, although you don't need psychological testing to determine PTSD.

A psychiatrist is a medical doctor who specializes in psychiatry, usually spending the bulk of training in psychiatric hospitals. Of the three, a psychiatrist is the only one who can prescribe medication. Being an M.D., a psychiatrist is also the most expensive.

Even if you think you need medication to help cope with your symptoms, you don't need to see a psychiatrist first. Any social worker or psychologist will consult with a doctor if it's needed, and refer you for possible medication.

It's not crucial whether you see a social worker, a psychologist, or a psychiatrist. What counts is whether you can work with the person. You also want your practitioner to be reputable. Having earned a license (and that's not an easy process), a therapist is accountable to the licensing organization. You have greater recourse if the therapist does something unethical. However, you cannot sue a therapist for not making you well.

PERSONALITY AND GENDER

Everyone has issues to work out, whether his therapist is male or female. If you've been raped, you may think you need to see a woman, but often seeing a man is helpful in showing you how to trust men again. Clients usually find that different issues crop up no matter whom they're seeing, and all are important to resolve.

Personality is more of an issue. Sometimes a client just doesn't like working with a certain therapist. As long as you're not running away from therapy altogether (switching therapists every two weeks because you don't like them is a form of running away), you may need a change. Some therapists simply clash with your personality. You're going to be unburdening yourself to this person, and you won't feel comfortable doing that if you find the therapist abrasive or arrogant. Some therapists are more direct than others; they ask many questions and make interpretations. Others sit back and let you struggle with the topics you want to bring up. Neither way is necessarily better. Some people don't like it if the therapist does more talking than they do. Others think they aren't getting their money's worth unless the therapist does all the talking.

It's okay to interview several therapists before you commit yourself to treatment. You should be able to get an idea of how warm they are, how direct, and how busy. You can ask the therapists how they might treat you for PTSD, but that's a hard question to answer without actually treating someone. A better question to ask might be what their experience has been in treating people with PTSD. You'll want someone who's familiar with trauma, but that doesn't mean they have to have suffered your same trauma. You can always join a support group of victim/survivors. What you need first is someone who knows what you're going through and how you can best recover. Experience in treating is equal to the act of surviving.

THE THERAPEUTIC EXPERIENCE

Therapy is designed to take you through the three steps of recovery. *The first goal is to make you safe.* Toward that end, the therapist may suggest medication—particularly if you're suicidal or severely agitated. Medication will reduce the symptoms of hyperarousal and depression.

The therapist may suggest a plan of action to secure your safety at home: a few days at a battered women's shelter, if you're in an abusive situation at home, or having a friend stay with you for a while if you live alone. Sometimes the therapist may show you relaxation techniques to help you manage your anxiety at home.

Contrary to what you might think, you will not unburden yourself to the therapist in the first few sessions. You will only give enough information to clarify your safety, once a diagnosis has been made. Relating your traumatic memories comes a little later. Your therapist will first want to ensure your safety and relative stability. Often a client is in a hurry and starts reliving memories before she is able to tolerate the pain they generate. Your therapist will want you to go slowly.

Remembrance and mourning comprise the second stage of recovery. Unfortunately, you can't get better without looking back at your pain, reexperiencing it, and then mourning. When you start talking about your memories, you'll find your intrusive symptoms increasing. The more you think about things and tell your therapist, the more memories will surface. Sometimes the memories come first; sometimes only the feelings come. In either event, you'll probably feel more scared, sad, or angry. A good therapist monitors your intrusive symptoms and slows down the process of delving into your past when you're becoming too stressed. One thing you should remember, however, is that no matter how gradually you recover your memories, you won't be functioning at your best during this time. Most of your energy will be going toward maintaining your stability during these painful times; be kind to yourself.

Although your job in therapy is to uncover the memories, sometimes it's wiser to put them aside until you're strong enough to face them all. That's called suppression, and it's a conscious act. You're not denying the feelings; you're setting them aside for the moment. As long as you eventually come back to them, you're not doing anything wrong.

Undoubtedly the process of remembering and mourning will be the hardest part of recovery. Some clients try to get around the pain by recalling the memories but not the feelings that went with them. You can't get better by keeping the two separate. To integrate your experiences, you have to reexperience the feelings. Think not only of what happened to you, but how you felt, what you heard, thought at the time, and smelled. Anyone can name a feeling; experiencing it is another story.

When I was in the hospital recovering from my son's stillbirth, I wanted desperately to make the feelings go away. At first the painkillers kept me sedated and asleep. But when I awoke, the emotional pain was there waiting for me, and I remembered every sensation that assaulted me. I could hear the cars driving by the hospital, and it occurred to me: people are going about their lives as if nothing is different! The sun had come up yet another day, and it was offensive to me. I would have preferred torrential rains. I tried not to think about our son. Every time I did, I felt my legs turning to ice. So many tears were bottled up inside my head that my sinuses throbbed with the effort of keeping them inside.

I was pierced with innumerable IV lines. Sometimes I'd tug on them, and the resulting sharp pain would take my mind off my son. An ice pack lay across my chest; once it burst open, and I lay soaked in ice water. I didn't tell the nurse; somehow, I thought the shock and discomfort was what I deserved. After all, I had unwittingly let my son die inside me.

Remembering what happened to you means remembering all those feelings again. It isn't easy. When I first shared these feelings with my therapist, I thought I could get away with just saying them. As my headache returned and the pressure behind my eyes grew, I realized I was trying to hold in the tears again. Only this time, I didn't have any IV lines to pull on to distract me. I had to feel that pain and shed those tears, and it was awful. But it was necessary to heal.

Remembering the traumatic experiences sets you up to mourn, which you must do to get rid of the trauma's hold on you.

Memories come back in the strangest ways. Some people start having flashbacks when their abuser dies; some people have flashbacks when they smell certain odors such as a certain cologne or the scent of wet earth. Many victims remember things when they find themselves in similar circumstances. When police notified Janet that they had arrested the man they thought had raped her friends, they asked her to come down to headquarters to identify him. One of the women had gotten a good look at the man, but Janet had consciously avoided looking at him. She couldn't identify him, but she had listened to his voice from the other room.

The police left Janet in a room at the station while they talked to different suspects. Janet sat in the dark, straining to hear what was being said in the other room. These were the exact circumstances she'd faced the night of the attack. She was afraid all over again, sitting in the dark, listening to another man's voice. Suddenly, she recognized one of the voices, and that whole evening came tumbling back into memory. Janet's reaction was so swift and so strong (she tried to run out of the room) that the police knew this suspect was their man.

Oddly enough, recapturing the memories and sharing them helps to put them into perspective. By telling your story out loud, you don't "lose the story," but you trade the shame and humiliation for dignity.

MOURNING

No matter what your trauma, you've lost something important. You might have lost all your possessions in a fire, your loved ones in an accident, or your belief in a safe, predictable world. People who survived Hurricane Andrew lost most of what they owned. Roofs were torn off houses and the contents blown miles away. Some people weren't insured and they lost everything they owned and everything they had worked on for years. Those who lived were grateful for their lives, but they had lost a lot, including their peace of mind.

Mourning is the hardest part of therapy. It hurts. Some people prefer feeling angry to feeling sad. Anger is often empowering; it makes you feel strong. Grief wears you out. Unfortunately, you can't let go of something until you've mourned it. Some victims and survivors refuse to mourn out of pride. They think they are standing up to their abuser by denying their pain. In effect, they're saying, "See? You didn't hurt me."

But the perpetrator does win if you can't be a whole person again. Reexperiencing all of your emotions is an act of courage and resistance. Survivors of the Nazi Holocaust against the Jews showed us just how horrendous their experiences had been by unearthing all their pain. Had they not mourned, we would not have understood the depth of their anguish.

Some people avoid mourning when they concentrate on getting revenge. Nothing anyone does can ever compensate for a harm already done; that harm can't be undone. You can't get back a loved one who has died; you can't get back your virginity; and you can't get back peace of mind. Victims and survivors often fantasize about revenge, believing that any victory over the perpetrator will erase the humiliation of their trauma.

One of my clients had been abused as a child by her father. At one point in therapy, she wrote a letter to her father's employer, describing her years of abuse at the hands of her father. Clearly, she would have gotten nothing out of exposing her father. In fact, it probably would have added to her embarrassment and powerlessness. What she really wanted was for her father to admit he had hurt her and wanted to make up for it.

Although she primarily wanted to hurt him, she also wanted him to validate her assumptions. She remembered being sexually abused at night, but it was a long time ago, and he never had acted during the day as if he'd done anything wrong. She wanted to hear from *him* that he had actually abused her. Since he denied it when she confronted him recently, she was furious at being rendered powerless a second time. "I can't make him admit what he did, but I can hurt him otherwise. I'll make him pay," she thought.

Nursing your injustice and waiting for your abuser to admit his wrongdoing are ways to hang onto the pain. Likewise, immediately forgiving your abuser or the person who killed your loved one is actually a way to avoid mourning. Some people tell themselves, "I've forgiven you," and think that's the end of it. It doesn't work that way. You don't need to forgive your perpetrator as much as you need to forgive yourself. Don't confuse embracing life again with embracing your abuser; they are not the same. Letting go of the hate, which binds a person to his enemy, doesn't mean you now like this person. You and your therapist can work out your feelings once you've brought them out into the open.

Reconnecting with others is the final stage in recovery. You've mourned your losses, and now you need to get on with your life. Humans were not meant to live isolated lives. People can handle so much more pain when there are others to share it. Some people have been so traumatized by their experiences that they don't know how to socialize anymore. Support groups are helpful at this point because basically you'll be looking at ways to get back into the community.

If you were abused as a child, this is the stage at which to challenge family secrets. My client would have felt better about herself if she had waited until after mourning her losses before trying to wrangle a confession from her father. At this point, as long as you're prepared for any outcome you're ready to come forth with your secrets. *The goal is to stop carrying the secret, not to convince the abuser of his wrongdoing.* You've known all along the abuse was wrong; you don't need him or her to agree with you. While an apology is nice, it doesn't erase the trauma.

A young woman wrote to advice columnist Ann Landers, complaining that her mother refused to believe that her stepfather had molested her. The mother then cut off all ties to the daughter, who still clung to the hope that Ann Landers could help make her mother see that this abuse had indeed taken place. Ann Landers' reply was, "There is none so blind as he who will not see." And that is true. You can't make someone believe you if he or she does not want to in the first place.

But you don't have to be a party to family secrets anymore. Once you get things out in the open (which doesn't mean you need to call your relatives, either), you lose your shame and humiliation. After all, what happened to you wasn't your fault.

A good way to reconnect with your community is through social action. Working to solve community problems such as missing children, drunk drivers, drug abuse, etc., is a positive way to use your energy. You're developing resourcefulness, initiative, and ties with similar people.

Your work is essentially done in therapy when you realize you can be happy again (which doesn't mean all the time), and you're engaged in healthy relationships. Your physiological signs of trauma will be under control (remember, you'll probably have setbacks with new stress) and you'll be able to tolerate your memories and feelings surrounding the memories.

For people with dissociative identity disorder, the therapist's job is much more complicated. In addition to helping the client mourn his losses, he has to help him integrate the different alters into one functioning person. Sometimes, that's not always possible, and the best the therapist can do is get the different parts (alters) functioning as a unit.

PROBLEMS IN THERAPY

Therapy is not a smooth process in which the client makes progress in an uphill fashion. More often that not, you take one step forward and two steps backward before you begin to move forward steadily. **Resistance** is a term therapists use to describe the client's reluctance to work on issues. Most clients, and many therapists, don't recognize the resistance at first. Some clients skip appointments, offering plausible reasons for their absences. Sometimes clients don't bring up important issues until they're winding up a session and know full well they don't have time to pursue that issue. Clients resist the most when they want to avoid their pain.

Transference is another issue that sometimes hinders and sometimes helps along the therapeutic process. Transference is when you have feelings for your therapist that you have for other authority figures. For example, Gina wore her shortest skirts and tightest sweaters to her therapy appointments. Having always related to men sexually in the past, she started doing the same with her therapist. Most of the time, transference issues cloud the therapeutic relationship. Clients tend to love their therapists (whom they see as rescuers) and hate them at the same time (because inevitably therapists fail to live up to their client's expectations). If a client doesn't resolve his transference from one authority figure (usually a parent) to another (the therapist), he'll simply get out of therapy when the situation gets sticky.

One client I saw years ago, Melba, stopped coming for therapy after she ran into my daughter and I at the mall. I saw her in the distance and waved hello. Melba interpreted my wave as a dismissal. She thought I didn't want her to come any closer to my daughter. So she stopped keeping appointments, and when I called her, she said she knew I was disgusted with her (which probably represented her own feelings about herself.) She didn't want to see me anymore. When I asked her to come in one more time just so we could talk about this, she brought her two-year-old son with her to the appointment. You can imagine how much work we accomplished with him distracting us.

The opposite thing happens when therapists have feelings for their clients that really reflect how they feel toward others in their lives. This is called **counter transference**. Sometimes therapists identify so strongly with your experiences, or maybe because you remind them of someone, that they attempt to do too much for you. They allow you to call them too often between sessions, or they make important decisions for you in session. These unlimited phone contacts may tell you that your therapist really cares about you, but orchestrating every move you make in your life actually works against you. The purpose of therapy is to empower you. If your therapist responds to your phone calls all the time, he allows you to rely on him instead of yourself. If your therapist thinks of you too much as a victim, he'll be more likely to handle problems for you that you should actually handle yourself.

Countertransference is something the therapist has to deal with himself; consulting with other professionals about his cases helps him work on any countertransference issues he might have. You just need to realize that a therapist who doesn't try to rescue you every time you think you have a problem is really doing you a favor. The greatest gift a therapist can give you is the knowledge that you can rescue yourself.

You should also be prepared for the possibility that you might be sexually attracted to your therapist, just as he or she might be sexually attracted to you. The therapist just won't act on this attraction, nor will he or she permit you to act on your feelings. A therapist with firm boundaries will keep you safe, and that's the most important thing a victim or survivor needs in order to recover.

Should your therapist cross this important boundary, you need to report him or her to the licensing organization. Someone there will investigate your charges. If you are too intimidated to do that yourself, find another adult you trust and report the sexual transgression. A therapist who can not maintain boundaries may traumatize all subsequent clients. He or she needs to be reported.

Your therapist serves you by listening to whatever it is you have to discuss. Sometimes, particularly with young children, the therapist just plays games or watches them play with toys in her office. Traumatized children reenact their traumas, and the therapist can make observations and interpretations by watching or engaging in the play. Sometimes, trauma victims don't have words for their feelings, or can't get at the words. Their therapist might suggest they draw a picture of how they're feeling. Art therapy is very helpful for some people who can't put their feelings into words.

Resolution to trauma is never final. Different stressors propel a person back into therapy. Someone who was abused as a child might resolve the trauma through therapy, but feel nervous all over again when her daughter approaches the age that she herself was abused. Some people manage to keep their traumas under wraps until their perpetrator dies. Then, all the memories return in force. Some people who have survived terrible natural disasters deal with their feelings by moving. If their children decide to move back to the area of the disaster, these traumatized individuals often feel a resurgence of their old symptoms.

So, therapy is an open-ended situation. You go through the steps of recovery, and you feel better. You don't have to stay in therapy all your life. If the symptoms return, you simply go back for some additional work, which doesn't mean going through the whole process all over again or for the same length of time. It's usually easier the second time around.

The goal of therapy is to help you find your integrity. For most people, the long, hard work is well worth it.

CHAPTER 9

Need for Hospitalization

Most people don't need to be hospitalized for the treatment of PTSD, but sometimes a person needs a more secure environment than what he or she has at home. Sometimes in the midst of therapy, a person becomes overwhelmed by all the memories and feelings and ceases to function. That's when others will consider hospitalizing him or her.

SYMPTOMS OF SERIOUS ILLNESS OR CRISIS

Any time a person is thinking of suicide, particularly if he has a plan and the means by which to carry out his plan, he should be hospitalized. It's impossible to keep another person safe when the person is in an unstructured environment and free to do as he wants.

If a person is hallucinating or hearing voices that tell him to hurt others or himself, he is out of touch with reality and needs hospitalization. If a person is unable to control his feelings and so is likely to harm someone else, he also needs a safe environment. And society needs to be safe from him as well.

Lastly, if a person is unable to function and unable to take care of himself, he either needs someone at home providing that care, or he needs to be supervised in a hospital. Hospitalization is a safety issue. If a person is not eating because he's too depressed to crawl out of bed, then he's in danger of starving to death. Hospitalization provides a structured and safe environment.

GETTING HOSPITALIZED

You would be admitted into a hospital by two means. You either willingly seek hospitalization (and you won't be admitted if doctors there don't think you need hospitalization), or you're brought to the hospital against your will.

To get treatment at a private hospital, whether it's a psychiatric hospital or a psychiatric ward of a general hospital, you need health insurance. If you lack insurance coverage, you might be eligible for treatment if a center has some beds set aside for nonpaying patients. Many places ask you to put up an initial deposit of $1,000 if you intend to make monthly payments on your subsequent bill.

Your other choice is to seek treatment at a community mental health (inpatient) center or the state hospital. These places have to accept even those unable to pay for their care.

More often than not, people who are suicidal or homicidal wind up in a hospital against their will. If a relative, or the police, think you're a danger to yourself or others, they can sign you into a hospital under an emergency order of detention. The hospital can hold you, even though you don't want to be there, for seventy-two hours.

After that, you'll have a court hearing where a judge will decide if you need further treatment.

The unfortunate part about being committed is that you have to pay for the treatment you didn't seek in the first place. One of my patients was committed to the hospital following a serious suicide attempt. Much to her distress, she didn't die but ended up committed to a facility—an expensive, private hospital in Maine. When she had improved enough to leave the hospital, she had incurred a bill for several thousand dollars. This bill was the final insult. She hadn't wanted our help in the first place, and now she was being forced to pay for it.

People who want to take their lives, or simply don't care to go on living, lack the judgment (according to the courts) to make decisions regarding hospitalization. More than likely, if people believe you're a danger, they can get you committed to a hospital for treatment. Then, you'll at least be safe. Whether or not you continue to receive treatment is up to you. Often people who are initially too distraught to care whether they live or die are relieved when someone else takes steps to secure their safety and well-being. Your therapist may recommend hospitalization for you at some point during treatment. It doesn't mean you have failed in your outpatient treatment. Sometimes the intrusive symptoms become too much to bear when you're in the second stage of recovery. Your therapist knows you'll be better able to handle these feelings if you're in a structured, supervised setting.

WHAT TO EXPECT IN THE HOSPITAL

The best thing about the hospital is that you have people looking out for you twenty-four hours a day. It's a safe environment. You may be in a psychiatric hospital or on the psychiatric wing of a general hospital. There are advantages and disadvantages to both places, but usually you end up going to the place that's most convenient and accepts your insurance coverage. If you want to continue seeing your outpatient therapist, you'll want to be hospitalized where he or she has hospital privileges.

If you're a suicide risk, you will probably be assigned to a ward with locked doors. The doctors and nurses lock the doors because they want to be sure you're safe at all times. They might put you under a suicide watch, which means someone will be checking on you every few minutes or watching you twenty-four hours a day. You may have to eat your meals in the ward, or you may go down to the hospital cafeteria. Hospital food isn't much different from the cafeteria food you've eaten at school.

Many hospitals employ some kind of system of gaining privileges. You earn escorted time off the ward, and then time off unescorted. You work your way up, sometimes in a matter of days, to day passes outside the hospital and home visits. Some places go more slowly than others to gauge your safety.

You will have some form of daily therapy. You will probably get to see your doctor (to update her on how you're feeling), but you won't necessarily have individual therapy with her each day. You'll probably have group therapy, art therapy, and time set aside for recreation. Hospitals structure your time so well that you hardly have a moment to sit around thinking about your problems. You will have an individual therapist, even if it's only someone who arranges for your release plans. If you've been seeing an outpatient therapist, he or she may come in to see you for therapy in the hospital. The hospital therapist will arrange your discharge with your family and your outpatient therapist.

Sometimes, doctors prescribe medication for you. If you're a danger to yourself or others, they can force you to take the medicine. People who initially resist may end up getting their medication as shots. Once the medication starts to work, judgment is usually restored along with calmer behavior. For suicidal patients, antidepressants are most commonly used. Antidepressants take about two weeks to work, although you might start feeling less tired, or more tired, in the first few days. Antidepressants have to build up in your bloodstream before achieving maximum benefits, so you may have to stay in the hospital that long to judge their effect. Some antidepressants cause you to gain weight, and with some, you'll have to follow a strict diet. Doctors don't always have the "magic pill" for your depression. They have to experiment with different doses as well as different types and it all takes time. As long as you're not a danger to yourself, you can always refuse to take the medication.

Most stays in a psychiatric hospital are not long. Insurance companies demand short stays, and doctors want you back out in the community as soon as you're able. To achieve this, doctors involve your family in treatment and assessing your support systems. Remember: the better your support system, the quicker you'll get better. Once you no longer need the structure of the hospital, you'll be discharged, and you can resume seeing your original outpatient therapist. Sometimes, you may have to seek hospitalization more than once to handle your symptoms of PTSD. Bad experiences are hard to confront, and you may require periodic hospitalization to keep you safe.

GETTING OUT OF THE HOSPITAL

The best way to get out of the hospital is to cooperate. When you've genuinely recovered, the staff will be glad to discharge you. How does the staff know you're better? Once you stop having suicidal thoughts or making attempts, and once your symptoms of depression, including low moods, lack of interest in your appearance, inertia, and lack of appetite, seem improved, the staff will consider you well. You don't have to come to terms with your traumatic past to be discharged. That usually takes a lot longer than the few days or week you'll need in the hospital. If you've been suffering from hallucinations, once those are gone or under control, you'll be ready for discharge.

The quickest way to get well is to participate in all the therapeutic activities. When staff members see that you're not isolating yourself, they usually consider you healthier.

Enlist the support of your outpatient therapist. Find out from him or her what should be accomplished prior to discharge. Everyone has a treatment plan that outlines the goals to be met for discharge.

You may try to fake getting better, but that's not a wise thing to do. The doctor may believe you and let you go, while you, the still-suicidal patient, may then harm yourself.

You can always request to leave the hospital. As long as you're not considered a danger to yourself or others, you can leave against hospital advice. That means the staff will let you go, but they don't think you're ready.

If you've been court-committed to the hospital, you can request a court hearing and attempt to convince the judge you're well enough to be discharged. Don't assume that a judge is in league with the hospital. More often than not, the judge is very much concerned with individual rights and will release you if he thinks you don't present any danger.

Don't try running away from the hospital. You already know you can't run away from your bad memories and feelings. Nothing is accomplished by running away from the hospital, either. You might discover that the hospital doesn't want you back just when you realize you really need to be there. One young girl I treated ran off from the hospital with a friend. We spent all that afternoon trying to find her or relatives who might know where she was. We finally found her and persuaded her to return, only to have her run off again the following week. Since she wasn't suicidal, we made no further attempt to get her to come back. Finding herself without shelter for the night, she returned to the hospital. But the admission staff couldn't justify her need for hospitalization and instead called her parents to come get her. The girl was angry that the hospital and "turned its back on her," but in reality, she'd turned her back on services first.

Hospitalization is just an extension of your ongoing treatment for PTSD. Sometimes you'll need more structure and supervision. If you view it as an aid in your recovery, you'll quickly see that it's not meant as punishment. In fact, hospitals can be very comforting places.

CHAPTER ◇ 10

Getting on with
Your Life

Whether or not you've used therapy to help you
heal from PTSD, at some point you're going to
be ready to get on with your life. The first thing
you need to do is trade in your victim status. If you see
yourself as a victim, then you haven't gotten over your
ordeal. You're no longer just a victim, you're a survivor.
You're still alive; you're still here.

Some people find therapy groups helpful at this point.
The best kind are the time-limited, issue-focused groups
run by professionals. You want to learn you're not alone
(there *are* others just like you), but you want to go beyond
merely telling your story and listening to theirs. Telling
your story to others is an important first step; you can't
skip it and move along to mourning. However, there's
more to healing than just telling the story. You have to
reframe your experiences and understand how things
went wrong. You can't do that initially; you have to have
progressed to the point where you're not blaming yourself

109

for the trauma inflicted. Then, and only then, can you put your behavior into perspective.

Therapy groups where everyone is in a similar stage of recovery are especially useful in helping you put things into perspective. You listen to everyone's experiences and realize the common threads in your lives. The point isn't to blame anyone for a particular trauma; rather, it's to look at what happened and to see how it might be prevented in the future. Traumatized people have a tendency to repeat their traumas, and abused people in particular have a tendency to hook up with unstable partners. Group members can point out problems to another group member more easily than therapists can. That's because they've been there, or are still there. Seeing group members further along in their recovery enables you to envision a positive ending to your pain, and sometimes helps you avoid the same pitfalls.

People learn from observing others. If you have two cotherapists running the group, you can learn a lot by watching how they relate. Dwain has run groups for sexual perpetrators for a number of years now. This past year he co-led a group with a therapist named Tanya, for sexual violence victims/survivors. For the first time, these women welcomed a male into their group. They learned a lot from the others in group, but also from watching Tanya and Dwain share leadership roles. Having a man and woman balance the power between themselves must have been a new experience for many of the group members.

Groups also show you how to give back to others. Being able to give to others helps you to receive as well.

SURVIVING

Sally, my former student whose car went into the river, never saw herself as a victim or a survivor. One day I asked my students to get together with others in the class and share something about themselves. At the next class we talked about the experiences. Another student mentioned what happened to Sally. I hadn't known about the incident. The whole class was in shock. Not only had it been a frightening experience, but Sally, who was so quiet in class, had emerged as a hero. It was amazing that she had the presence of mind and courage to pull her son out of the van and jump into the river.

My other students couldn't stop talking about Sally's experience, and Sally began to look at it in a new light. She hadn't thought of herself as a survivor, someone who was strong. But the more she realized she had survived an incredible ordeal, the stronger she got in other areas of her life.

If you've survived a terrible ordeal, remember above all: you have to be strong to survive.

BEYOND SURVIVING

Now this may sound like contradictory advice: you don't want to think of yourself as a survivor forever. And why not? After all, isn't surviving a trauma a good thing?

Of course, seeing yourself as a survivor is better than seeing yourself as a victim. A victim has things done to him; a survivor rises above those things. Survivors are strong, and you've been strong enough to put your trauma into perspective. The problem is continually thinking in terms of the trauma. When you call yourself a survivor, whether you label the trauma or not, you're still defining yourself in terms of the trauma. At some point, you've got to get back to being just a person—not a victim, and not a survivor. Having survived an ordeal should not be the first thing others know about you. You are a person first.

My friend with the rancorous divorce used to tell everyone she met that she'd survived a marriage made in hell and a divorce that was worse. People got tired of hearing about her experiences. After a couple of years and several months of therapy, she stopped dragging the divorce and her survivor status into every conversation. At the same time, she started to live again. When she was no longer defining herself in terms of the failed marriage, she was no longer tied to an ex-husband who had dominated her life. By dropping the victim and survivor images, she effectively dropped him from her life. She was ready to move on.

TAKING CONTROL

When something awful has happened to you, it's easy to feel out of control. That is why it's important to regain control of your life as soon as you're able. First, take steps to recover (making yourself safe, remembering and mourning your losses, and putting them into perspective), and then set positive goals to get on with your life.

Maybe you need to get out of a painful marriage. Maybe you need to join a social action group and work toward changes in the laws. Maybe you need to move to a different part of the country. Moving away from a disaster doesn't mean you're running away from your trauma. Sometimes, it's the smartest thing you can do. Making positive changes in your life means you're willing to take a chance on the future.

Janet moved away from California after the earthquake. She wasn't running away from a traumatic experience; she was making a safer environment for her children. She doesn't lie awake nights now, worrying when "the big one" is coming. She took control of their futures and confronted her fears.

If you seek legal restitution, be sure you can live with any outcome. Just because you know that you deserve restitution doesn't mean the courts will see it that way. Life isn't fair, and sometimes you don't end up getting the amends you deserve. But seeking restitution is a positive step; it says you're worth seeking justice for.

If you've been raped, it's not enough to heal. Learn to protect yourself. A gun is not always the solution; more owners than criminals get hurt by guns. But if you get a gun, make sure you know how to use it. Or learn martial arts such as tae kwon do or karate, because in addition to learning to protect yourself, you gain a feeling of strength. Even if you don't want to learn a form of martial arts, you can take a self-defense course or a rape prevention course. A strong person is one who doesn't simply rely on others to protect her; she takes steps to protect herself.

If you were sexually abused as a child, protect yourself and keep your own children safe. Never leave a child alone with a known perpetrator.

HANDLING NATURAL DISASTERS

If you've survived an earthquake, a hurricane, or a tornado, you might think there's nothing you can do to protect yourself in the future. Natural disasters are not predictable. If you're like Janet, you may want to move away from earthquake country or tornado-prone areas.

But even if nature isn't totally predictable, we still have things we can do to ensure our safety. Meteorologists can forecast tornadoes and hurricanes. If you know conditions are right for one to develop, or one is already on its way, take steps to protect yourself and your home. Know the safest places to hide during a windstorm (either the center of your house away from windows, or the northeast corner). If you're directly in a hurricane's path, board up your windows. Then leave your house and move further inland.

If you are traveling through another state and the sky looks threatening, keep your radio tuned to a local station. That way, you'll be warned in advance if a tornado has been sighted in the area. Know to get out of your car in a windstorm. Either lie low in a ditch or hide under a bridge underpass.

Of course, you can't predict an earthquake. If you live in an earthquake-prone area, make sure you know the signs of an earthquake and where to seek shelter. Have an escape plan should an earthquake happen in the middle of the night. Keep your house equipped with flashlights and fresh batteries and stocked with extra food and water.

OTHER DISASTERS

Learn how to drive defensively. Assume no one else knows how to drive, and be prepared for someone to do something stupid. If you give up driving after an accident, you're still just as liable to be involved in an accident as long as you're in a vehicle.

If you've survived a fire, make sure you know what caused the fire. If the wiring was faulty in your house, have it checked by a professional. Keep smoke detectors on every floor, and periodically check that the batteries are working. Never wind down with a cigarette when you're sleepy. It's too easy to fall asleep with a lit cigarette.

Realize you can't totally control your environment. Bad things do happen to good people, and bad things can always happen again despite your best attempts to guard against them.

DOING SOMETHING POSITIVE WITH YOUR ANGER

Use your anger positively. It takes a lot of energy to keep memories repressed, and it takes a lot of energy to stay angry. Put that anger to other uses. Get involved in changing the laws or helping others survive a similar trauma. Start a support group.

Go back to college for a degree in one of the helping professions. People who have survived traumas and have taken the time to heal are excellent helpers. Take some time to explore your interests.

If you want to get your mind off your past (and you're working on it in therapy), try learning something that forces you to concentrate harder than usual. You can't keep reflecting on your traumas when you're in the middle of a handball game, for example.

Taking care of yourself also means knowing your own limitations. When you're too immersed in your own pain, you're not in a position to help other people with their problems. You are not mentally strong enough to take on their burdens as well as your own. That doesn't mean you have to push them away; rather, you should refer them to a professional. Taking care of yourself sometimes requires putting your mental health ahead of others' problems. There is someone around who can help them; it doesn't always have to be you.

GETTING BETTER

Keep a journal if you're going through hard times. Writing down your thoughts and feelings often helps you make better sense of them.

Write everything down, especially your feelings, and don't leave out the bad stuff. Otherwise, how will you know when you're better?

Someone once said, "Time heals all wounds." You might think that person is crazy, or that he'd never suffered a loss. But time does make the pain more bearable (as long as the grief isn't buried). And after a time—usually a long time—the pain lessens.

Another person once said, "Living well is the best revenge." If you can survive and hold your head up, you have your self-esteem. Your trauma didn't take that from you. And that's the definition of living well—maintaining your dignity and worth.

Epilogue: When Someone You Know Has Suffered a Trauma or Is Diagnosed with PTSD

1) Learn all you can about PTSD. Read books about your loved one's particular trauma, as indicated in the *For Further Reading* section at the back of this book.

2) Let your loved one, friend, or relative talk. Don't discourage him or her from talking about the trauma. It is a release to talk even if she ends up saying the same stuff she told you yesterday. She may wind up crying, but *you* haven't made her feel bad. Mourning losses is a painful process; victims need to feel the loss before they can let go of it. However, don't tell her she ought to be crying. Let her cry as she wishes.

You'll probably hear a lot about the trauma. That's because the trauma doesn't go away with just one telling. You're doing your friend a tremendous favor by listening. Don't underestimate your kindness, and remember that mourning losses is a very long process. Try not to set a time limit on it.

3) Don't listen if you can't give the victim *all* your attention. Here are other things to avoid:

- Cutting the victim off before she finishes what she's saying.
- Comparing similar events in your life; pain and trauma aren't comparative.
- Don't play psychologist; refer the victim to a real psychologist.
- Don't judge or belittle; the victim only needs you to listen and doesn't need to hear what you think he or she did wrong.

4) Expect your friend to have good days and bad days, but don't tolerate inappropriate behavior. If your friend is using her trauma as an excuse to be rude and mean, point it out and demand better. You're doing the victim a favor by pointing out unacceptable behavior such as swearing too much, ranting and raving at store clerks, or hiding out in his or her room.

5) Seek to understand how your friend feels about the trauma and the future. If he can share his feelings with you, he's acknowledging them to himself.

6) Understand the importance of victims' support groups. These group members have been through the same or similar traumas. Understand the importance of community support and recognition.

7) Set limits on what you can do to help your friend. Even therapists have to set limits. People who have been chronically abused often tend to exhaust others with their dependence and resentment. Refer them to their therapist, or contact them yourself, when you're in over your head.

8) If the victim sounds suicidal, report it to a therapist, teacher, minister, parent, or other appropriate adult. Your friend needs help at once.

9) Don't expect your friend to get better in any set time. People heal differently. Don't put pressure on the victim to conform to *your* expectations. If things are dragging on with no signs of improvement, suggest she see a professional. Then let the professional and your friend handle the progress.

10) Encourage your friend to think positively about his future. Let him know that you believe things will get better. And if all else fails, help him plan that future. Just remember, as a friend and loved one, you don't have to do it all. You just need to be there.

Glossary

alters Separate and unique systems of personality; two or more develop in an individual with dissociative identity disorder.

antidepressant Medication used to treat PTSD when it is complicated by depression.

beta-blocking agents Medications used to treat PTSD victims. They control a person's physical reactions when a person has to face similar stress repeatedly.

competence One of Erikson's developmental tasks; it means being good at something.

constriction Leading a restricted life to avoid dealing with further trauma or reexperiencing pain.

countertransference The complex feelings a therapist has toward his client in therapy.

deficiency needs According to Abraham Maslow, a person's basic needs for survival, security, attachment, and self–esteem.

delusion A belief that is contrary to reality, but is still held firmly.

dissociative identity disorder Disorder in which an individual splits into two or more distinct personalities, called alters, who help the host personality cope with trauma.

dissociative state Trance-like state to which trauma victims resort to keep from being aware of their current trauma.

flashbacks Memories that draw the victim back into the scene of the original trauma, as if he were experiencing it all over again.

growth needs According to Abraham Maslow, a person's need to learn, appreciate beauty, live up to your potential, and lead a spiritual life.

hallucinations Seeing or hearing things that are not there.

hyperarousal   Being vigilant and always on the alert for danger.

initiative   One of Erikson's developmental tasks; it means being able to start things on one's own.

insomnia   Being unable to fall asleep or stay asleep.

intrusion   Having the memory of a trauma continue to reinsert itself into one's consciousness either through nightmares, flashbacks, or daydreams.

paranoia   Symptoms of delusions and loss of contact with reality.

perpetrator   Person who commits a crime or an abuse against someone.

psychophysiologic signs   Physical ailments, such as stomachaches, that mimic the victim's reaction to the initial trauma and continue to occur in times of stress.

reenactment   Reliving through behavior, usually play, of the original trauma.

regression   The unconscious act of reverting to an earlier time in one's life that seemed safe, and then behaving as if one were that age.

rehearsing   Thinking or talking about a memory.

repetitive dreams   Dreams similar in themes or exactly alike in details that one has after a trauma.

repression   The unconscious act of forgetting a painful memory.

resistance   Victim's reluctance to deal with issues in therapy.

rigidity   Behaving in a set fashion, usually to avoid situations reminiscent of the trauma. Also, a deadening of the emotions and a loss of playfulness.

suppression   The conscious act of not thinking about something painful.

transference   A client's feelings for his therapist that often reflect his feeling toward other authority figures.

trauma   Frightening event out of one's usual human experience. It may be a life-threatening event or the experience of witnessing death or injury.

Help List

HOTLINES

National Child Abuse Hotline
Childhelp USA
800-4-A-CHILD

National Coalition Against Domestic Violence
800-799-7233

Town National Crisis Line:
800-448-3000
800-448-1833 (TDD for hearing impaired)

Youth Crisis Hotline
800-448-4663

Ottawa Sexual Assault Centre Hotline (Canada)
613-234-2266

Ontario Coalition Rape Crisis Center (Canada)
705-268-8381

INFORMATION/REFERRALS

National Organization for Victims' Assistance (NOVA)
1757 Park Rd. NW
Washington, DC 20010
202-232-6682

National Rehabilitation Information Center
800-346-2742

National Self-Help Clearinghouse
25 West 43rd St., Room 620
New York, NY 10036
212-354-8525

National Victim Center
800-FYI-CALL

Victims of Violence National, Inc.
Unit 2, 220 Mulock Dr.
Newmarket, ON L3Y 7V1, Canada

WEB SITES

About Trauma
http://gladstone.uoregon.edu~dvb/trauma.htm

This is the best web site to launch from to get more coping tips on dealing with trauma, and also to read up on symptoms and treatment.

For Further Reading

Anderson, Terry. *Den of Lions*. New York: Crown Publishers, Inc., 1993.

Gold, Mark. *The Good News About Panic, Anxiety and Phobias*. New York: Villard Books, 1989.

Hearst, Patricia, with Alvin Moscow. *Every Secret Thing*. Garden City, New York: Doubleday and Co., Inc., 1982.

Herman, Judith Lewis. *Trauma and Recovery*. New York: Basic Books, 1992.

Hunter, Mic. *Abused Boys*. New York: Fawcett Columbine, 1990.

Hybels-Steer, Mariann. *Aftermath*. New York: Fireside/Simon and Schuster, Inc., 1995.

Kotlowitz, Alex. *There Are No Children Here*. New York: Doubleday, 1991.

Levi, Primo. *If This Is a Man*. New York: Summit Books, 1965.

O'Brien, Tim. *In the Lake of the Woods*. New York: Houghton Mifflin Co., 1994.

———. *The Things They Carried*. Boston: Houghton Mifflin/Seymour Lawrence, 1990.

Terr, Lenore. *Too Scared to Cry*. New York: Basic Books, 1990.

———. *Unchained Memories*. New York: Basic Books, 1994.

Waite, Terry. *Taken on Trust*. New York: Harcourt Brace and Co., 1993.

Wolff, Tobias. *In Pharoah's Army*. New York: Alfred A. Knopf, 1994.

Index